To Peter

The Humming Bird Nest

Journey of a Lifetime

fllow workers

for Jsees

God bress,

Halry + Aj

All profits from the sales of this book
will go towards impoverished
SEAN programmes such as to the
Mapuches, Wichi, Enthlit, or
prison ministries, etc.

PEGGY BARRATT

The Humming Bird Nest

Journey of a Lifetime

SEAN International

Apologies, Acknowledgements & Dedication

IN WRITING this book, my biggest regret has been that, because of the very multiplicity of colleagues and friends to whom we are deeply indebted, many have not been mentioned by name, especially those in Paraguay, Argentina and, after our retirement in 1981, in England. To have done so would have confused my readers and defeated the purpose of the book which is to make our story in South America as readable as possible.

For the same reason, I also stop short of featuring the enthusiastic activities of our twenty-one grand and great-grand-children (which would have been unending!) except for one incident which must represent all that the others are doing to carry on our work now we are retired.

To all these dear grand-children and friends, my sincere apologies and most heartfelt thanks. I dedicate this book to them, to my five children and especially to my beloved husband of 60 years, Tony, without whose tireless help this book could never have been written.

Peggy Barratt

Contents

CHAPTER ONE

Drainpipe romance

WALLOP! MY eyes streamed with tears. It was a cold winter's evening as I stood on Strawberry Hill Station with Tony Barratt, a young student from Glasgow Veterinary College. He was a very new friend who was staying with us over the weekend. He was demonstrating enthusiastically how someone had hit someone else on the nose. Sadly he misjudged by a fraction his distance and caught me right between the eyes. Covered with confusion he poured out apologies. 'Oh, that's all right' I blurted out from behind streaming eyes, 'I didn't mind a bit, really I didn't', just as if it were a daily occurrence to be punched on the nose.

These were dark days when the regular, heavy air-raids of the Second World War were at their height. We were on our way to a youth club for disadvantaged kids, near to Vauxhall Bridge. It was some relief from the horrors of the raids to see the lives of many of these youngsters being reconstructed and their obvious relish for the varied club activities on offer. Tony and I had a common interest in such projects.

As we prepared for the return journey about 10 p.m., the air-raid sirens started to wail, soon followed by the all too familiar pulsating drone of the enemy bombers overhead. On enquiring, we discovered to our dismay that all train and bus services had been cancelled. However, with the optimism of youth (I was seventeen and he twenty-one) we set off, in spite of the blackout, to walk the long miles back to Twickenham.

At first, whenever the whistle of bombs seemed too near, we dived for the nearest cover. However we soon realised that at that rate we would never get home, so with a brief prayer we decided to run the gauntlet – Clapham, Putney, Barnes, Sheen, Mortlake, Richmond... then over the bridge and all along the Thames tow-path in a cold, damp mist, and so back to Twickenham, my home. At last, about 3.30 a.m., weary and footsore, we staggered up to the door.

Once previously when I had been locked out, having forgotten the key, I managed to scale the drainpipe and climb into one of the up-stairs windows. So with a hearty boost from Tony I was just about to reach the window when my mother's voice came floating down: 'Peggy, is that you, dear?' Tony's

courage failed and in panic he let me go. Unsupported, I shot down the drainpipe on top of his head. At that moment romance struck.

My mother called out 'I'm coming down, dear'. I saw Tony stiffen as he anticipated the worst, but she was her usual sweet self. She trusted us both implicitly and was only thankful that we had got back safe and sound.

In the morning Tony had to get up early to catch a train to Taunton to 'see Practice' for the rest of his vacation. This was the way in which students gained hands-on experience in a veterinary practice. I sent him off with a special breakfast of bacon and eggs, thus blowing at one go my family's full week's rations. I knew my dear parents wouldn't mind them being used for such a good cause!

Our romance was wonderful but far from easy as we were hardly ever together. Tony was either seeing practice when on vacation or else at college in Glasgow during term time. However, we realised that we were far better off than those many couples who were separated with their men-folk serving overseas. We built up our relationship by post; Tony wrote to me daily, usually on the old tram he had to take; I replied daily. It was on this meagre fare that our love had to thrive.

The rare occasions when we were able to be together were in Strawberry Hill where I was living in the home of my best friend Rosemary Farrer, to me always known as 'Roro'. I was helping her mother by looking after ten-month old twins that she was fostering. It was one of the most interesting households I have ever known; it just buzzed with activity. 'Ma' Farrer had filled her large home with a collection of extraordinary characters; these were some of the Jewish refugees that were pouring into England from Germany. There was a Dutch sea-captain, a medical doctor and his wife, an Austrian girl and a dear little five-year-old German boy called Walter who had lost all his family in the concentration camps. Finally there were Sigi Nissel and his silversmith father, Nunki.

3

To take our minds off the horrors of the war and of the bombing they used to organise the most delightful musical evenings. Roro played the cello, her brother Mick the piano and I sometimes scraped away on my violin. How seventeen year old Sigi stomached this I shall never know; he was a most brilliant young violinist – in fact he later became one of the members of the Amadeus String Quartette; he was none other than the now world-famous Siegmund Nissel! As Tony's parents lived just round the corner from us in Strawberry Hill it was at one of these social evenings that we first met. Here he invited me to go out with him, the journey that terminated in my rather undignified descent upon the unsuspecting head of my future husband.

CHAPTER TWO

Early years with my vet

WHEN WAR broke out, Tony had enlisted in a Scottish regiment, 156 Low Field Ambulance. However, he was soon discharged to continue his studies as a vet. This was a reserved occupation, as agriculture was fast becoming our only food supply. In spite of the severe rationing, the U-boat blockade of our island was threatening the population with starvation. He qualified two years later.

He was offered his first post as an assistant in a practice in Suffolk that proved to be most unsatisfactory. To start with, it meant we had to be parted again. As we were not yet married, he had to leave me behind in Twickenham. We'd really had enough of separation during his college years in Scotland. Furthermore, we soon discovered that his new employer was a chronic drinker and often out of control.

Although he was only earning £5 a week, we both decided it was high time to get married. He was given the Easter weekend for our wedding and honeymoon. We met up at his parent's home in Strawberry Hill to pick up a few papers, and then went on to my place in Twickenham. We were married on Easter Sunday at St. Stephen's Church, Twickenham. My bridesmaid was my life-long friend, 'Roro'. The church was packed with young people from our respective youth clubs, along with family and friends. It was a wonderful service.

Mummy decided to have our wedding reception at home. She worked extremely hard to make this a success with the help of our family and neighbours. I can't think how they managed on the meagre wartime rations. Later, Roro remembered the occasion with these words, 'Peggy's eyes matched her lovely blue dress and jacket. I had conjunctivitis, so mine matched my pink dress!'

We, the honeymoon couple, stayed the night at the Star and Garter Hotel on Richmond Hill where we had to put two pennies in the gas meter to warm the room up. Our wartime supper was liver and onions followed by prunes and custard! But in our state of euphoria it tasted delicious.

After breakfast the next morning, we set off for Suffolk. We arrived in the afternoon when Tony was sent straight out on a case. His lodgings had a nice double room so he had made arrangements for both of us to live there. I immediately started to work half-time in the kennels, but later got a full-time job in the office of the local sugar-beet factory.

Tony's main job was to drive his employer around to his cases, and then from pub to pub where he got steadily more and more sozzled. This was not why he'd spent five long years of training in a veterinary college. About the only vet job he remembers doing was the highly dangerous one of castrating unbroken colts. Adverts for assistants in those days would invariably stipulate 'Only apply, if can castrate standing'. This was a most barbarous affair, as no anaesthetic was used. The unbroken colt was led into the stable and forced against a wall. What was known as a 'twitch' was used for counter-irritation; this was a pole with a loop of cord at the far end. This cord was put on the sensitive upper lip and screwed up tightly, causing considerable pain. The idea was to distract the animal from what you were doing at the other end.

One had to approach gingerly from the head end, because an unbroken colt was extremely dangerous and would lash out with his hind legs. With a sharp crescent-shaped knife, he had to slash the scrotum and pull out the testicle on its cord. The cord was crushed to prevent haemorrhaging. Then the whole process had to be repeated on the second testicle. However abhorrent this practice was, as an assistant Tony had to do what he was told. The alternative would have been to lose his job and that would not have been a good idea with a new young bride to support.

We stuck it as long as we could but were so disillusioned that at the end of the year we began looking for another post. A good one came up, advertised in the Veterinary Record. It was in Ashbourne, Derbyshire with a salary of £12 a week, quite an improvement on what we had been earning. We applied, were accepted and in due course arrived at the door of Mr. Peach's establishment. They were rather old-fashioned premises but in a strategic position in the central square. As there was no house going with the job, we had to live in digs once more.

The practice was set in the most gorgeous countryside. Both the Peak District and Dovedale were a comfortable drive away. Then there was the little village of Ilam, where Isaac Walton wrote his famous tome on fishing. We had the occasional outing together to enjoy this beautiful scenery.

As my part in the war effort, I got employment in the subsidiary branch of the Rolls Royce Factory. Here I had to inspect the screws and bolts for the aeroplane engines. Recently, I was chuffed to learn that these were the now famous Merlin Engines. They made such an impact on improving the quality of the Spitfire, that defended our shores so effectively, that they helped to turn the tide of the war. For his part, Tony was coming to terms with the climate. The winters were appalling and farms were often cut off by deep snow. Following the snowplough, he would often be the first to reach an outlying farm, even before the doctor.

Because of the rugged nature of the terrain and the steep hills on which the animals grazed many of the cases he saw were extremely serious and distressing. Not even in hilly Scotland had Tony seen the like. Often a calving cow would be out days, even a week, before the farmer spotted her. By this time, of course, the calf would be dead and all the uterine fluid gone. So when he was eventually called, he would be confronted with a dreadful situation. With his arm up to the shoulder in the dry uterus, the pressure of the cow straining was crippling. A dead calf would often have to be cut up, piece by piece within the womb, with an embryotome. This was a sturdy metal tube with a loop of cutting-wire at one end. By sawing on these wires at the outside end, a necrotic limb could gradually be severed from the dead calf's body. Last of all, the dead calf itself could be pulled out with cords. I sometimes had to join in, and pull on these cords as well.

There still remained the danger of a retained placenta. After a dead calf, this would be putrid and attached like a limpet to the hundred or so cotyledons that lined the inner surface of a cow's uterus. It was a long, unpleasant job, as the placenta had to be detached from these, one by one. The stench of removing a rotting placenta was insufferable. Also, the subsequent staining of the operator's arm was most unsightly, as it was virtually impossible to remove by scrubbing. Tony always used his left arm for this task, as it was less conspicuous on social occasions.

His garb for doing these jobs was basic to the extreme; in those days there was none of the efficient protective clothing worn by our modern vets. He would strip to the waist, tie an old sack around his waist with a bit of binder twine and, sometimes lying in the snow, just get on with the job. At the end, he would often be offered a bucket of freezing cold water to wash in. As he would be covered in slime and faeces, one can only imagine his condition as he drove home.

Some of the routine jobs Tony had to do as a vet had their drawbacks. For example, one day when I was sitting on his knee, I idly turned up the collar of his jacket and to my horror it was teeming with lice. 'Well', he said 'I often felt as if something was running through my hair when I was listening to a cow's chest, but I thought I was imagining things.' In our practice the farmers thought it was a bit sissy for the vet to walk about with a stethoscope around his neck. I brushed the lice off in the garden and from then on Tony decided to use his stethoscope, come what may, so we never had a repetition.

Very early on, Tony was called to a cow with a prolapsed

uterus. The grossly swollen womb, hanging out, was massive. It was his job to get it back into the cow's body. He had never seen this done, so all he had to go on was what he remembered reading in his sanitised textbooks. So he concluded that it was just a matter of brute force. But the more he struggled the more the cow strained and the less progress he made. At last, totally exhausted and baffled, he wisely decided to phone for Mr Peach to come and help.

He quickly arrived on the scene and set about his task with his usual efficiency. He was a brilliant and most practical vet, a great, powerful, beefy man; that is why Tony called him, thinking that with his strength he would give one, mighty push and the womb would slide neatly back into place. Nothing could have been further from the truth. While the cow strained, he gently held it where it was. When she relaxed, he pushed, but only an inch, holding what he had gained when she began to strain again. So, inch by inch, over a prolonged period, the huge lump gradually began to reduce in size. Then, at last, with an impressive surge, the whole heavy mass slid back and disappeared from sight inside the cow. After this brilliant demonstration, Tony never again had trouble replacing a prolapsed uterus.

He was now entrusted with sewing up the lips of the vulva, the outer orifice to the uterus. This, of course, was to prevent the womb from falling out again. A stall in the cowshed was prepared to receive her; an old door, built up at one end with bales of hay or straw. The cow was placed on this, so that her hindquarters were higher than her head. After several days, when the womb had finally settled down, the door was removed and she was put on the level again. Once her stitches were removed she recovered perfectly.

Another time, we were called out to put a ring in the nose of a very overgrown bull, reported to be unmanageable. The plan was to secure the bull's head by pulling it up to a beam with a long rope, tied securely around his horns. Tony was on the other side of the hayrack with the punch and ring at the ready. I stood outside the open door to shut it if required. The farmer was inside, ready to pull the rope. All went well until he began to do so, when the bull objected; he reared up and brought down the beam and all. 'Shut the door' Tony shouted. This I did, but remembered just too late that the farmer was still inside. He took an Olympic leap over the half door, landing in a pile at my feet. Only Tony and the bull were left inside, eyeing each other suspiciously. At that, Tony, who didn't want to spend the night with the bull, decided to call it a day and yelled for the farmer to let the bull out.

It was decided to sedate the bull with Chloral, a powerful

tranquilliser. As this was very bitter, they withheld all water for a day, so that he would be really thirsty. We then give him a bucketful of water to which had been adding a stiff dose of Chloral. This did the trick and Tony was able to ring him without further difficulty. Sadly they found that, even with the ring, he was too big and vicious and so had to be sent for slaughter.

The Ashbourne practice was a really tough school with a very steep learning curve, but Tony's time with Peach gave him experience such as he could never have gained elsewhere. For this he was eternally grateful. At the end of the year I was expecting our first child and we decided to look for a place that was offering a home of our own. It was also a time to think about seeking a partnership. Again relying on the Veterinary Record, we came across an advert from a practice in Falmouth offering a house for the assistant. As it was with prospects of a partnership, we applied and were duly offered the job.

The owner of the practice, a Mr. Smythe, was a brilliant vet; he had been a lecturer in London Vet College. Mrs. Smythe was warm and friendly, but rather lonely. I was very fond of her and also of her two young sons, Peter and Richard. We began doing everything together: the shopping and taking the children to the beach. The Smythes' house, with the surgery attached, was well situated, high on the hill looking over the estuary of the river Fal. On the other side of the water we could make out St Just-in-Roseland and St Mawes. Our house was just round the corner from the surgery. It was spacious, with a fine bay window in the sitting room from which we had a great view over the harbour.

In Falmouth, I was able to go out on occasional cases. Some of the places were especially beautiful such as the Helford Passage. To reach St Mawes we had to cross the Fal estuary on the King Harry Ferry. I so much enjoyed both these outings.

Here the breeds of cattle were quite different from those in Ashbourne. There they were mainly black and white Friesians, here they were nearly all Jersey or Guernsey herds. The milk was so rich, and the cream on the top of the bottles so thick, that we really did have to watch our waistlines. There were, of course, the usual calving cases. But again so different from Ashbourne as here there were usually live calves to deliver. As the ground was flatter, there were no more prolapsed uteruses and the week-old rotting placentas were largely things of the past.

We were certainly enjoying green pastures. The only blot on the landscape was the attitude of the Cornish farmers to a newcomer. Like most farmers at that time, those in Cornwall were very conservative. They disliked being visited by a new assistant, however experienced. By sheer force of habit, they would insist on having the boss, and only the boss. 'Sorry, Sonny, no way are you touching my cow' was their usual crusty greeting on a first visit, especially as Tony looked young for his age. When this occurred, he would politely climb back into the car and reverse slowly towards the gate. 'When will Mr. Smythe be out?' would be the invariably anxious inquiry. 'Sorry, Gandpa, he's very busy, I doubt whether it will be this week' – this as he continued to back a little further towards the gate. 'Well, will you just have a look at her then?' Sensing a chink in his armour Tony would reply strategically, 'If you have no confidence in me, what's the point?' and then graciously relent. Once he had delivered a healthy calf, they would sometimes even ask for him next time!

It was in an attempt to level the playing field as regards the farmers' initial prejudice against his youthful looks that Tony resorted to a rather dubious subterfuge. Urticaria in the cow was an acute allergy. Overnight, the whole body could blow up alarmingly. The cow's face would be so inflated that it resembled a hippopotamus. However, it would go down as fast as it had come up. For a new young vet, desperate to impress a cynical farming community, this was an opportunity too good to miss. When he heard such a case described over the phone, he would leap into the car and drive at top speed to the animal before it had a chance to get better on its own! An injection of a mild tonic was sufficient to effect a miracle cure! If he had delivered a healthy calf after a really bad presentation, he'd scarcely get a thank you; it was expected. But this was something different; his fame would now spread far and wide! 'That young vet may be a townie but he's brilliant' was their verdict. May my husband be forgiven; my only excuse for him must be that he was still very young.

It was here that Terry was born. He arrived safely in February, delivered by Tony's great-aunt whom we called Aunt Daisy. She had also delivered Tony twenty five years before. Our parents visited us to join the celebrations, as did many of our friends; they were all a great help. When Terry was three months old, I was feeding him at night, and peacefully looking over the harbour when suddenly all hell was let loose. Rockets, fireworks, guns and sirens all blasted off together. He nearly jumped out of his skin. The war with Germany was over. It was unbelievable and our hearts were full of gratitude that at last the bloodshed in Europe was over.

By our second Christmas in Falmouth, the farmers, with whom we now got on really well, were most generous. We received eggs, Cornish clotted cream, a goose, a cockerel. Then we went down with flu' and couldn't even look at any of it!

Happy as we were with our work in Falmouth, we were getting more and more uneasy at the way things were turning out. Mr. Smythe had made no move to offer us the promised partnership. Increasingly, I was being left alone at night when Tony had to deal with all the emergency calving cases. Having to remain on call, we never had a weekend free when we could go to church together. We longed to have at least some time for youth work, sport and the occasional recreation together, so perhaps the moment had arrived to start up a small-animal practice of our own.

CHAPTER THREE

Our own vet practice

NOW WE had left behind the agreeable life in Falmouth we had to decide what our next step would be. It was an unexpected encounter in Ilfracombe, on the North Devon coast, which eventually decided us to settle there. We had met the Rev. Guthrie Clark, the local vicar, and he had a relative in the veterinary profession. When visiting Guthrie in Ilfracombe, he had observed, 'If I were a bit younger, I would set up practice here; there is such scope.' So Guthrie persuaded us to consider doing this ourselves.

Our decision was helped by the fact that my parents had just arranged to rent a large, country house in Ilfracombe with the idea of converting it into a guest-house. This was called 'Score House' and was situated in a beautiful valley just outside the town. It had a nice big garden, a small lodge at the end of the drive, and stables. My parents, thrilled at the possibility that we might move near to them, did all they could to help. Daddy offered to convert the stables into kennels for our practice. We could live in the lodge, at least until we became established.

We now began to look for suitable premises in which to set up a small-animal practice. In the window of an estate agent we spotted just such a place on offer. It was over Barclay's Bank, and owned by them. As it was ideally situated on the main street we went to enquire. At first I thought that the bank manager looked rather severe. However, as we told him of our plans for a veterinary practice, he became quite animated and said that he was sure that we would be able to come to some agreement. In fact the bank would paint the interior for us, to give us a good start.

The property had a large downstairs room, with a plate-glass window giving onto the street, ideal for a waiting room. Up a little flight of stairs was a toilet and wash basin. More stairs led to two good-sized rooms, one suitable for a surgery, the other for our pharmacy. We immediately saw the possibilities and said we would take it.

Tony's Dad had promised to lend us a capital sum to set up the practice, so now we could begin getting the surgery ready. In all our previous practices, the waiting rooms had been rather austere and dreary; we wanted something much brighter and more welcoming. First we painted the old linoleum emerald green and laid on it two brightly coloured coconut mats. We bought some ex-army metal chairs on the cheap and painted them. On a rod over the plate-glass window, I hung a pale green net curtain. Attractive magazines, such as the Lady and Country Life were laid out on a table. Finally, I filled a large vase with copper-beech leaves. Today this kind of thing is standard, but then it was breaking new ground.

We began ordering our stock of medicines and the latest equipment. Many of these were only just coming out and were very exciting. Finally, we bought our car. The proud day dawned when for the first time we were able to put up our plate; A.J.Barratt M.R.C.V.S. At last we had our own practice.

As vets were not allowed to advertise in those days, we had to find other ways of earning a little money while we waited for our first patients. Tony began writing articles and got quite a few published in the Small-Holder, Country Life and others. Some then asked him to write regularly. Once we had our first patients, word spread rapidly. Then the R.S.P.C.A. asked us if we would become one of their official clinics, the practice was finally up and running.

One of the reasons for limiting our practice to small animals was to give ourselves time to get involved again in youth work and sport. On arrival in Ilfracombe, Tony immediately joined the town cricket club. Before long, he and Guthrie Clarke, the vicar, were opening the batting regularly. Most weeks there was a write up in the daily paper about all their exploits on the pitch, sometimes with a photo. Of course, this all helped in the growth of the practice.

However, the most significant event, relating to the cricket, was meeting Douglas Milmine at one of our matches. He had come to watch Guthrie play, as he was his new curate. We immediately hit it off with both Doug and his wife, Rosalind (or Ros for short). We formed what became a lifelong friendship as they were to follow us to South America and would play a major role in the development of the work there.

Along with the cricket went the youth work. Tony and Doug worked together on this. First they built up a strong team of young associate leaders, both men and women. The objective of this leadership team was to recruit at least one representative from each school in the town. When we held a 'squash' with plenty of games, good food and fun, our reps were encouraged to invite all their friends from their school. The result was phenomenal. By the time we moved on, there were a good hundred regular club members. Quite a few of these later became leaders themselves, some in the UK, others in needy parts of the undeveloped world.

Sport was a real feature of the club. We set up and trained a table tennis team that performed and excelled in the local league. Another more unusual but popular sport was archery; the Grammar School kindly lent us its grounds, thanks to the headmaster who was also in the Ilfracombe cricket team.

Meanwhile we had to attend our regular clinics, perform frequent operations and visit sick animals in their homes. We also had some rather unusual emergencies, of which one was a foxhound puppy brought in by the Master of the Pack. One of the horses had trodden on his paw and it had been badly crushed. Usually it was better if the owner wasn't present, but this fellow especially asked if he could help. I was assisting Tony, giving the anaesthetic, when there was a tremendous crash. The Master of the Pack, all six-foot-two of him, had measured his length on the floor! I now had two casualties, a swooning man and an unconscious puppy so I gently kicked the human legs out of the way so that I could get round the operating table to the puppy. Eventually the man came round and sat up, so I gave him a glass of water to drink, while we finished plastering up the injured leg and paw.

Tony loved the surgical side of small-animal practice; we set aside at least one day a week for this and I would help him. Usually the two grannies were only too glad to look after our two-year-old son, Terry, on these operating days. However, when this was not possible, we had to bring him with us. On these occasions he was so good and patient, sitting in his high-chair, most of the time nodding off.

One of the operations that became something of our speciality was the neutering of three-month-old female kittens, called spaying. This was not just a fad but a serious attempt to cut down on cruelty and thoughtlessness. So many unwanted kittens were destroyed callously by drowning. This operation meant happy cats and carefree owners. No more unwanted kittens and no more coming into heat with the tiresome attentions of dozens of tomcats.

In those days, small-animal practice was considered to be very much the poor relation of veterinary work. The profession was almost entirely geared for large animals, especially the horse. However, things were just beginning to change. New drugs and techniques were becoming available, such as antibiotics, penicillin and Nembutal. Furthermore, a distinguished surgeon, Professor Wright, was pioneering new operating techniques; one of these was a much-improved method of spaying small kittens. Tony had been taught this by one of Professor Wright's students. By this method, he would remove the uterus and both ovaries through a single, minute incision in the flank, avoiding the danger of postoperative shock. On coming round from the anaesthetic, a kitten would start jumping around just as if nothing had happened. Previously, a large incision in the abdomen was needed, to reach both ovaries.

As yet, this technique was not widely practised so, once the news got round, clients began coming in from near and far. One lady, a breeder of valuable Siamese cats, would send four or five female kittens in at a time that didn't come up to her standards for breeding. They came in baskets in a taxi all the way from Bideford, the other side of Barnstaple. When spayed, we would return them in the same taxi.

This procedure was greatly facilitated by another fresh advance; a new anaesthetic called Nembutal. When injected in the vein, the animal just fell asleep; no more struggling, no more deaths from heart failure. This revolutionised surgery and also euthanasia (putting terminally-ill pets to sleep painlessly). Mind you, it took considerable skill in getting an intravenous needle into the vein of a three-month-old kitten when this vein was little bigger than a button thread.

Another regular client was a man who raced greyhounds. He frequently came to the clinic with the same problem, a dog with a swollen toe joint. This was always on a toe that was on the inside of the track as the dog rounded the bend; it placed excessive pressure on that joint. We had a good success rate by amputating the affected toe above the inflamed joint. After a good period of rest, most patients could race again.

On another occasion Tony was called out to see a large and ill-tempered Setter. It had a disgusting mouth, caused by the build up of tartar, and this had resulted in badly infected gums. His breath was terrible. Moreover, he wouldn't let Tony near him. His owner was a clergyman in a parish near Combe Martin. Tony decided that the safest way to get the job done properly was under an anaesthetic. He calculated from the dog's weight that the dose would be thirteen capsules of Nembutal, mixed in his food. The clergyman politely, but adamantly, refused. Thirteen was an unlucky number and no way would he submit his pet to such a risk! We couldn't believe that this gentleman would let superstition deprive his pet of medical attention that would have given him such relief.

One night at 3 o'clock in the morning we had an urgent telephone call from the police. An old lady had been trapped in her home with a mad Bull Terrier. Could the vet attend and do something about it? Tony made his way to a block of old tenements down by the harbour. He climbed up the dimly lit stairway and knocked on the door. A very dishevelled old lady peered round the half-opened door. In the darkness Tony could just make out a bloody rag wrapped round her arm. She had obviously been badly bitten and was extremely agitated.

She pointed towards one of her inside doors from which emerged a series of fierce growls. Tony cautiously eased the door open just a crack. The mad dog sprang at his throat but he managed to slam the door shut just in time. However, he was badly shaken. He paused to weigh up the options. Through a half-open door, there was no way in which he could get a dog catcher (loop) round the beast's neck in order to restrain it and put it to sleep humanely. There seemed only one thing for it; to use a deadly poison one-drop of which in the mouth would bring down the strongest dog. He reluctantly loaded a syringe. When he edged the door open the mad Bull Terrier sprang at him again, but this time he was ready. As it snarled in his face, he squirted the poison in its mouth. The poor demented creature dropped like a stone. Tony returned home in a really distressed state of mind; it had all been a horrible experience.

We had an even more tragic event, but at the opposite end of the spectrum. From a mad dog we now had to attend to dear little Paddy, my close friend for over seventeen years. When I was about eight years old, Daddy bought me a little puppy. She was biscuit-coloured and looked very like a little Cairn Terrier. I called her Paddy and proudly presented her to everybody as my 'thoroughbred mongrel'. As I didn't have a brother or sister she was to me the next best thing. In the war, when the raids first started, I got so fed up with going down to the shelter that in the end I used to stay in bed; Paddy would sleep under the eiderdown with me. From the sound of the engine, she could tell which were the German planes. When she heard them she would press up under my arm and when they had gone, relax again. She took no notice of our planes.

She had always been very fit and had lovely litters of puppies which always seemed to come in twos or fours; for these we found good homes. When she reached this ripe old age of seventeen she developed severe kidney trouble and we didn't want her to suffer any longer; so we sadly decided to put her to sleep ourselves. We gave her a Nembutal capsule in a bit of mince and she curled up on my lap and went to sleep. When Tony gently injected a bigger dose of Nembutal, she never even stirred; she just didn't wake up again. We were so comforted to know that her end had been peaceful. We buried her in the grounds of Score House, where my parents lived.

We always had the hope that one-day we would be able to serve abroad. With these thoughts in mind, Tony felt it would help if he trained for ordination. When we finally got to Chile, this, along with his veterinary qualifications, gave him far more scope.

Before taking such a big step, we felt we needed a clear sign from God. We would only leave Ilfracombe if someone we could really trust came forward to take our place in running the practice and caring for the flourishing youth work. About a year before, we had a delightful visit from Major Ken Davis who had just been discharged from the army veterinary corps. He had heard of our practice and was interested to see what was going on. We got on really well. Now he wrote to us: 'I am willing to pay any price for your practice'. As he shared all our aspirations, we knew that this was the sign we had asked for. Ken Davis, his wife Susan and little baby Peter arrived in Ilfracombe in time to look after the practice and allow Tony to go to college. They stayed with me as paying guests. I continued to help Ken in the practice, as I had done with Tony. He was able to pay cash down for the good will of the practice. This allowed us to pay back the money Tony's Dad had lent us to set up in the first place.

At the end of the Easter term, Tony was torn in two directions. Our second baby was due at the very same time as he had to sit his exams. If he missed these, he would have to repeat. What should he do? We talked it over and agreed that he ought to sit them. Both lots of parents were near and Tony's Auntie Daisy, who had delivered Terry, would again attend the birth at home.

Tony sat the exam, ran to the station, jumped on the train, and got to Ilfracombe at 6.30 p.m. where I met him with a very excited Terry – excited to see his Dad but even more excited to see 'Thomas the Tank Engine', the steam train. We had a hug and hurried up to the engine for Terry to see it. Suddenly there was a shrill blast from the whistle as the driver opened the steam. Terry must have jumped a foot in the air, and that was a pretty good jump for a boy of four. He burst into tears with shock. After consoling him, we went home to supper, put Terry to bed – and labour began. Early next morning Terry came and knocked on the door to say goodbye to me. He was going to his little friend for the day. As Auntie Daisy was of the old school she wouldn't let him in to see me. I was so touched, therefore, when I suddenly saw his Rainbow comic being gently pushed under the door. It was his way of saying goodbye. Rosemary was born that day around mid-day on 12th March, 1949. We named her after my best friend, Roro. It was a very thankful and proud Dad who was there to celebrate with us. He'd just made it. At the end of the year Tony successfully passed his final exams and we were all set for the next phase of our lives, now with a family of two.

In describing these vet years, I have had to keep myself well in check; otherwise, the whole book could be taken up with sick animals rather than with our years in South America. However, for those who are interested, one of our successors in our

Ilfracombe practice, Cameron Gibson, under the pen name of Alexander Cameron, has written some excellent books describing what happened to our practice after we left. His books have had a huge circulation both in the UK and even more in the USA. They continued treating small animals, but also now built up an extensive large-animal practice, including many interesting cases in the local zoo.

For several years the Ilfracombe practice kindly sent a donation of 10% of their profits to our work in Chile. This helped to tide us over when for a while our station allowance was so small that it was impossible to run the large mission on it without outside help.

CHAPTER FOUR

Letter from South America

HAVING PASSED his college exams, Tony now started to look around for a good place to gain initial experience in our new work. Once more it was Guthrie Clark who stepped in and altered the course of our destiny! He and Doug Milmine, with their families, had moved together from Ilfracombe to Slough. They had a large working-class population and an Industrial Estate to look after; it was also near to Heathrow Airport. Guthrie now invited us to join them.

For Tony, in some ways Slough was rather a step back from our Ilfracombe days in the sense that he and Doug Milmine saw far less of each other. Doug was in charge of a large housing estate while Tony was the assistant curate working with Guthrie in the centre. So whereas in Ilfracombe they had worked so closely together in building up the youth work, now they had separate responsibilities.

For me, on the other hand, Slough was just a continuation and deepening of the wonderful relationship that I had enjoyed in Ilfracombe with Mrs Clark and Ros Milmine and their families. There, I had revelled in the warm family life we all enjoyed, now it was a matter of building on this foundation. Our little group of mums and kids was soon to be joined by two more families.

One day I answered the front door and there was an American lady who greeted me with 'Hi! My name is Dorothy Churchill'. That was the beginning of another life-long friendship with her and her family; like the Clarks, she also had four children.

The fourth mum to join our group was Mrs. Myrtle Skinner with her five children. Her husband held a top position in the I.C.I., a giant pharmaceutical and paints company. They had a large house on the outskirts of town where her hospitality knew no bounds. By the most astonishing coincidence, we discovered that Tony's Auntie Daisy had brought both the Skinner and the Churchill children into the world, just like ours.

For me, and I think for all the others, Margaret Clark was a real role model. All her four children had been adopted and they were a very happy family. She had a companion help, Doris Piper, who had been accepted as one of the family and remained with them until her death quite recently. Although Margaret kept open home for all visitors she was always unruffled, always welcoming. She taught me how to cater on a shoestring for any number of people and how to share our wartime rations with others. We all helped each other with the children.

Our growing family lived in a nice little house, right opposite a cherry orchard and on the road out to Stoke Poges. It was only about two hundred yards from the Clark's large vicarage further down the road. I loved the situation. The small garden backed on to an enormous cemetery. This was appropriate, as Tony had to take an incredible number of funerals. These did give him an insight into the heartaches of bereavement and the chance to offer comfort and counsel. In complete contrast, there was also an unending stream of weddings to take.

Hilary, our third baby, was born on Whit-Monday bank holiday. Tony had planned to take a group of young people for a ramble. When I suddenly went into labour in the night, Doug kindly volunteered to take them instead. Hilary was born in our home, at ten o'clock in the morning, with our doctor and Auntie Daisy in attendance. All went well with the actual birth of our new little daughter but then things began to go badly wrong; the afterbirth was partially retained and haemorrhaging began. The doctor phoned for an ambulance. I was rushed off to the Royal Canadian Hospital in Taplow. Meanwhile, baby Hilary had been hastily wrapped up in a towel and put in the ambulance with me. All the time, the doctor was pressing on my stomach, trying to stop the bleeding. At first I was unaware that anything was seriously wrong but on the way I began to realise how grave things had become. In the ambulance I was asked my blood group and amazingly I remembered it; I had been told this for the first time recently at the clinic. This proved to be life saving, as I was Rhesus Negative.

I rapidly got weaker and weaker from the loss of blood and on arrival at the hospital was rushed immediately into the theatre for a transfusion. Now there was consternation; they were unable to raise a vein because my blood pressure had fallen so low. How they solved the problem I shall never know; the next thing I did know was that I was coming round in a lovely little room with a window looking out on to a beautiful garden and the sun streaming in. I was filled with a great sense of joy and peace.

Now a further problem! Apparently, in all the confusion, no one had taken responsibility for putting a name tab on baby Hilary. This, of course, should have been a routine procedure. So there was near-on panic among the staff because an unnamed baby had turned up wrapped in a towel and nobody could trace where she had come from. Eventually she was brought to me. I knew immediately that it was Hilary because I had seen her for a brief moment in the house before we had left. At last she received her name tab around her wrist and all returned to peace and calm. I spent ten days in the hospital having transfusions. When I was discharged and returned home I was fine. Also I had Tony, Terry and Rosemary to help me look after baby.

It was also in Taplow that the All Nations College was situated at that time. Following the Clark's example, we kept open house for the students. As they were away from their own homes, I think they really appreciated this. Several of these students later played an important role in our work in South America. For example, on graduating from the college, Bill Flagg went out to Chile, to manage the farm in Quepe.

One of Tony's principal duties in Slough was to be chaplain of the Boy's Brigade. He greatly enjoyed working among the young people again; it took him back to our happy Ilfracombe days. Here we made further contacts that would bear fruit in the future. One of the Skinner boys, Brian, was among the smartest lads on parade. Later, he joined us in Chile, where he succeeded Bill Flagg as the farm manager in Quepe.

We were now coming to an end of our time in Slough and began to look around for a situation where we would have more responsibility. Once more our concern for people in countries that had not enjoyed the benefits and privileges that we had, were increasingly preoccupying us. This was weighing so heavily on Tony's mind that he felt he should get down on his knees and ask God for some direction. At that very moment the early post arrived, so I took it in to him. 'Look' I said, 'There is a letter from Chile. Whoever do we know out there?'

We opened the letter and Tony started to read it out. It was from Bill Flagg, the student from All Nations College. As he had been just one student in many, we had temporarily overlooked that he had gone out to Chile. 'Look' Tony laughed, 'He is asking us to join him there. He says our veterinary skills would be invaluable, especially on the farm he is running in Quepe.' Tony paused to think. 'The last place on earth I want to go to is South America. The Roman Catholic Church is so strong there and I don't want to be competing with them all the time'. We looked at each other sceptically. Then Tony suddenly burst out, 'But hang on a minute, I was just asking God to guide us as regards our future work. Can we really dismiss this so lightly?' We were chastened. What was the good of asking for God's guidance, if the moment we received it we laughed it out of court?

So we began to take this letter from South America more seriously. We continued to pray about it and the more we did so, the more convinced we were becoming that this was the right course to take. Finally we offered our services to the society that had sent Bill out; it was the South American Missionary Society, known affectionately as 'SAMS' for short.

From then on things moved with breathtaking speed. They were desperate for a replacement in Chol Chol where the missionary in charge had just left without notice. Could we be ready to go immediately? We knew nothing about Chile. Tony confessed, shamefacedly, that he didn't really know exactly where it was on the map. There were passports to get, equipment to purchase and family and friends to bid farewell.

It was then that we met a young Australian clergyman, called Allen Yuell. He was a friend of Douglas Milmine and he had an unusual story to tell. When still a curate in Australia, he had pulled an old magazine from his rector's wastepaper basket. It contained an article written by Doug that greatly impressed him. Now he was visiting the UK and so had sought Doug out. As Tony was full of our projected journey to South America, he asked Allen if, once back in Australia, he could awaken interest there; this he promised to do. In the excitement this soon passed out of our minds but in the event it had far-reaching implications; on our first home leave, Tony was invited to visit Australia to report on our work and to seek to interest them in it.

We had a wonderful send-off from Slough at which Tony was presented with a saddle; this because in Chile much of his visitation would have to be done by horseback. The local press was there and took a photograph of Terry, perched on the saddle, that appeared in next morning's paper; but by then we were well on our way.

CHAPTER FIVE

Journey into the unknown

THE 14TH of November 1952, our departure date, dawned at last. Our great friend, Douglas, drove us to Waterloo station where we were to catch the boat train to Southampton. There we were due to board the liner 'RMS Andes' on our first voyage to South America. I was really excited by the enormity of the challenge before us. At the same time the responsibility of caring for the three small children weighed heavily upon us both. Terry was seven years old, Rosemary three and a half and little Hilary still just a baby of eighteen months. Our other two, Patricia and Jonathan, were born later in Chile.

The pressure began to mount even before we had left the shores of England. At Southampton docks all five of us had to wait in a queue that never seemed to end. To the children this must have felt like an eternity. By the time we had got on board and put them to bed they were so restless that it didn't take much to upset them. For example, while I was shaking out Terry's pyjamas he lent back on a hot radiator with his bare bottom. It was only a touch but he let out a yelp that would have raised the dead. When I inspected the damage I saw it had left six nasty red wealds. Although I immediately applied a soothing cream these remained with him for days.

Baby Hilary went straight off to sleep. So did Rosemary at first but in the middle of the night she suddenly woke up in a panic, sobbing her heart out as she had had the most awful nightmare. It was all due to a story that a rather insensitive aunt had read her about a 'Scissors Man' who would snip off her

28

fingers if she sucked them! So it was a dreadfully disturbed night, not only for us but also for an elderly couple in the next cabin. Understandably enough they kept thumping on the dividing wall. The final indignity came when they called the steward and demanded to be moved to another cabin, as far away from us as possible! It certainly was not the most auspicious start to our new ministry! In fairness to our erstwhile neighbours, they were charmingly forgiving when next morning they learnt of the mishaps that had caused all the disturbance. We noticed, however, that they didn't ask to return to their original cabin!

Unlike Tony, I had been abroad before. As a young child I had lived for a year in Lisbon. Mummy had been born there when her parents were working in the cork industry and when I was only four she had returned with me to visit her family and I suppose to show me off! We stayed at the flat of her parents, Grandpa and Granny Barley at 6 Rua Pineiro Chagas. This was on the second floor of a huge block just down the hill from the army barracks. Each morning at breakfast I would hear the clip clop, clip clop of an approaching horse and I would run out on to the balcony to see a mounted cavalry officer approaching. The second time this happened, the officer smartly saluted me and so I saluted back. From then on this became a daily routine. The kindness of this cavalry officer to a little girl of four years old was typical of the attitude of most Portuguese. They were rightly famous for their love of children.

As Lisbon was our next port of call, I just couldn't wait to visit it again. So once we had docked there we all swarmed off happily enough, eager to see the city where I had once lived. Fearful of pickpockets, Tony had buttoned our passports away inside his jacket. His anxiety was increased when on boarding a tram with Hilary in his arms he found himself seated hard up against a rather scruffy looking workman. 'Probably a builder' I thought, noticing the folding ruler sticking out of his pocket.

The man began showing an interest in baby Hilary by smiling and chucking her under the chin. With this, I could see Tony stiffen and tighten his grip on our passports. At last our ordeal came to an end and, as we alighted on the pavement, the tram drew off. Then, too late to remedy the situation, we saw to our horror that Hilary was triumphantly clutching the poor man's beautiful folding ruler in her chubby fist. Unable to return it to its rightful owner, we kept that ruler in our family as a salutary reminder that one should always be slower to judge a person by their outward appearance than by their inner worth. So it was that a very chastened missionary family re-embarked, now harbouring within their ranks a budding pickpocket of quite outstanding talent.

When it came to the ceremony of crossing the line poor Tony was the last to receive the heavy-handed treatment meted out by Neptune's henchmen (two excessively beefy sailors). Whether by luck or design we don't know but we suspect some quisling leaked the information to them that Tony was a clergyman. This became self-evident when King Nepture roared out, 'Ah! My kingdom and yours don't mix, so get him lads'. After a good ducking, they proceeded to pour the entire bucket of treacle over his head and then followed this up with an ample dusting of white flour.

At approximately 3.45 p.m. on Tuesday the 27th November 1952 we sailed into the magnificent bay of Rio de Janeiro. This first contact with South America was both awe-inspiring and symbolic. The majestic entrance to the bay, sparkling in the sun, opened up before us, filling our eyes and hearts with deep emotion. As the RMS Andes slid gracefully into the harbour we were struck by the exuberance of the natural beauty. The immensity of the emerald green mountains, the clear turquoise sky and deep blue sea, were so much more than any of the picture post cards we had previously admired.

And there before us, etched starkly on the wonders of creation, were our human efforts: to the front, magnificent skyscrapers, mansions and beaches of the rich and to the rear, clinging to the hills, the deplorable squalor of the 'fabelas' or

shantytowns. Over both, with arms outstretched, towered the giant statue of Jesus, a stone icon to so many but to Tony and me it pointed, however dimly, to our wonderful, risen Lord Jesus, the one whom, above all others, we so much wanted to share with the people of this continent. As it was still light, we took photos of both the Sugar Loaf mountain and also of the fantastic Corcovado (hunchback) mountain, crowned with this world-famous statue of Christ.

It so happened that at this time a well-known evangelist, named Dr. Edwin Orr, was attracting vast crowds and was seeing the most remarkable scenes of spiritual revival as a result. To Tony and his friend Douglas Milmine, Dr. Edwin Orr was the 'Billy Graham' of their period and as such had become one of their heroes. As they had heard rumours that he might be in Brazil sometime, they had often speculated together on the possibility that our arrival in Rio would coincide with one of his visits there, even giving us the opportunity to hear him preach. However, they recognised that this would be highly unlikely. Nevertheless, Tony had promised to let Douglas know if anything did transpire. So leaving Hilary on board in the care of a kind friend, our little troop set off happily to explore Rio, but nothing was further from our minds than Dr. Edwin Orr.

After some shopping, we were all walking down the Avenida Rio Branco when a man put his hand on Tony's shoulder and said 'Excuse me, are you a Protestant minister from England?' It was Dr. Edwin Orr! Seeing Tony's dog collar, he knew that he was some kind of cleric, the fact that he had a wife and two children showed he was certainly not a Catholic priest and our accent had betrayed our English identity.

Considering that this world-renowned preacher could have been anywhere in Brazil, if not the world, it was nothing short of a miracle that he should accost us in this highly unconventional way on a busy street in Rio de Janeiro. After all, we were complete strangers to him. Furthermore, coming on the very first day of our arrival in South America, we took this as a sign from our great God that he approved of the commitment we had made to serve him in this continent. We certainly had something to report back to Douglas, our good friend in England.

Dr. Orr proved to be a charming person. Although he only had one day in Rio he obviously wanted to take our little family under his wing. He insisted on introducing us to one of his favourite restaurants where he treated us to a luxury tea. Then we all took a taxi to the airport to collect his luggage and finally dropped him off at his hotel. We really were sorry when finally we had to bid him a very fond farewell – especially Terry who had been captivated by his thrilling stories from so many countries around the world.

Feeling a bit flat, now that our kind new friend had gone, we decided to cheer ourselves up by taking a trip up the Sugar Loaf. This has twin peaks, the first rising to a dizzy height but the second being even worse! We had never seen heights like these before, far less had we gone up them. To ascend the mountain, we had to take the aerial railway, a tiny capsule suspended in thin air high above Rio by a thread-like cable. It worked in two steps, the first from ground to the lower peak, the second scaled the summit of the Sugar Loaf itself.

With some trepidation we all clambered into our capsule along with other passengers. Soon we were hanging high above Rio. By now it was night, so we could see all the lights winking up at us far, far below by which we could just discern the outline of the beach and bay. There was our ship, the Andes, at anchor and all lit up. Finally, and most magnificently, the wonderful statue of Christ was brilliantly illuminated as if hanging on its own, high in the night sky.

Suddenly, Rosemary began to sob inconsolably. We naturally thought that the altitude had affected her and so we sought to comfort her accordingly. 'It's all right, Rosy; it really is perfectly safe'. 'But we haven't got Hilary with us' she sobbed. 'And we're going to Jesus without her'. The mighty statue of Christ, high on the neighbouring Corcovado, and all lit up, had made a tremendous impression on our little three and a half year old girl. We realised again how true are the words, 'A little child shall guide us.'

We sailed down the coast to the giant capital of Argentina, Buenos Aires, where our first and abiding memory was that Eva Perón had died recently. In her memory, her husband, the dictator Perón, had ordered all public clocks to be stopped at the exact moment of her death. The city was in a state of tension; no one knew what to expect. The members of the English community were especially jittery and were wisely seeking to keep a very low profile. As newcomers, we were blissfully unaware of all this. As a consequence, when Tony was later travelling on a bus with an English companion, he innocently enough pointed up at one of these clocks. 'Why are all the clocks here out of order?' he enquired in an all too audible voice. 'For goodness sake shut up!' his companion hissed between clenched teeth, 'It's more than our life is worth to point and speak like that.'

Our hand luggage, which had to last us the two days train journey across the continent until we reached Chile, passed through customs without incident. Our main luggage was banded up and labelled 'En Tránsito'. On the train we were unable to afford meals in the dining car for our five so I had brought a big tin of Fray Bentos Corned Beef and an ample supply of delicious Argentine bread, plus a few biscuits and cheese. After a struggle with the key, I succeeded in opening the Corned Beef, only to find that the fat had melted in the intense heat. Without plates or cutlery, it was almost impossible to eat. Eventually, I had to spread it, like butter, on the bread.

The thing that saved us was the steaming cups of hot milky coffee and rolls that the steward brought round for breakfasts. But this wouldn't do for little Hilary. We had been told that on no account should we drink the water or milk unboiled so I couldn't even make up her baby food. All we could think of was some orange juice. So we turned to our trusty Spanish Dictionary, probably at the time our most valued possession! For 'orange' we got 'naranja'; for 'juice' we found 'jugo'. Putting these together, with some trepidation we asked for, 'Jugo de naranja, por favor!' (juice of orange, please). No doubt our accent let us down as our request was met with an expression of blank incomprehension. Then, suddenly light dawned, and he replied brightly, 'Oh, Orange crooosh' and produced bottles of fizzy orange drink. Poor Hilary's face was a picture when she took her first sip of what would have to be her only drink for the rest of the two days on the train. Mercifully, I had put a packet of disposable nappies in my hand luggage; at least these made baby's journey a little more comfortable than would otherwise have been the case.

After 36 hours of dusty pampas and the terrifying heights of the Andes, our train finally puffed into Santiago station, the capital of Chile, at 1.30 in the morning. In a 'hotel' of sorts any hope of sleep was soon dashed by a dance band playing through the rest of the night.

We still only had our meagre hand luggage and the clothes we were standing up in. I was therefore delighted when after breakfast we were taken to retrieve the rest of our luggage which was 'En Tránsito' from the customs. Alas, we were told that it had not yet arrived in customs. Furthermore, as it was Saturday, everything would be closed over the weekend. Then the final blow – Monday was a national holiday so it was no good returning before Tuesday.

So on the Tuesday we eagerly returned to the custom's shed only to be told that no luggage had yet arrived. But not to worry! If we returned 'Mañana' (tomorrow) it would certainly have done so by then. This we were soon to learn was the secret of the eternal optimism of many South Americans – 'Mañana' was the simple, and most convenient, answer to their every problem. Wednesday our luggage had arrived – but had not yet been unloaded from the train! However, once again, it would be quite all right 'Mañana'. Finally, on Thursday morning we were greeted with a triumphant 'Your luggage has arrived'. Sure enough, there it was waiting for us. At last their unwavering optimism over the past week had paid off and clearly they now felt fully vindicated! We had certainly arrived in the continent of 'Mañana'! The friendly custom's official took everything out of our bags. After all, that was his job. However, he soon gave us the all clear. Once we had re-packed we were at last free to take the train south to our final destination.

After another cramped and tiring overnight journey we arrived in Temuco where we were warmly welcomed by a small band of retired missionaries who had settled in Chile. Among them was 85 year old Canon Wilson, affectionately known as 'Daddy' Wilson. In 1895 he had started to work in Chol Chol, our final destination. He was a grand old Scotsman, in the tradition of Dr. Livingstone, who had faithfully served the indigenous Mapuche people in the Chol Chol area for most of

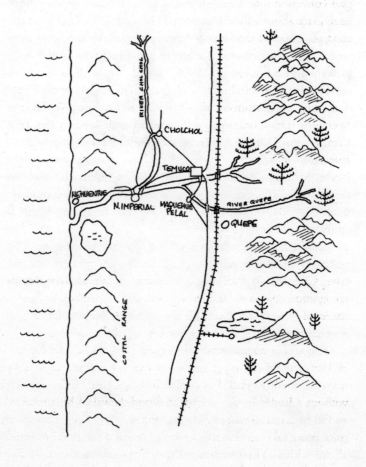

his adult life. On the death of his first wife, he married Miss Strugnel, known to all as 'Struggles'. Although retired, he now joined her in her caravan ministry to the Mapuches. Together, they travelled over a vast area in an old ox-drawn caravan that she had converted into a mobile medical clinic. They would stay in each place about a month at a time. Then the Mapuches from the next place would send a yoke of oxen to pull them over to their 'reduction' (reservation), a scattered group of straw huts (rucas) governed by a Cacique or Chief.

The name 'Mapuche' means literally 'The People of the Land' and they were indeed the original inhabitants. When the Spaniards (Los Conquistadores) invaded their land in the 16th Century, the Mapuches were the only indigenous group not to surrender. It was only with the introduction of intoxicating liquor that they were eventually seduced, not by force, but in this insidious way. So, one of the sad and all too common sights in Chol Chol was of Mapuches filling the cantinas and coming out drunk.

Although the descendents of the Spanish invaders are now popularly known as 'Chileans', in fact the Mapuches were the true Chileans. It was to help them in their struggle for recognition that our Society was originally formed under the name of 'The Araucanian Mission'. (Note: 'Araucanian' is the foreigner's name for the Mapuches).

The whole community worshipped the ground that 'Daddy' Wilson walked on, most of them having benefited personally from his medical skill. His centre in Chol Chol had been left without a leader by the unexpected withdrawal of his successor and so his most urgent prayer was for a younger man who could once more take up this responsibility. A few days later, he shared all this with us. Then, turning to Tony he confided, weeping, 'You are the answer to all my prayers. Now I can depart in peace'.

As Temuco was the provincial capital it was here that we would have to apply for our 'Carnets' (Identity Cards) which everyone living in the country had to carry at all times on their person. As Quepe was much more accessible to Temuco than Chol Chol we were now taken there. So for the next fortnight we would be shuttling back and forth between Quepe and Temuco.

Quepe was the home of Bill Flagg. You may remember Bill was the one who had written to prompt our move to Chile. In Quepe we were now able to plan for the future with him. He especially hoped that Tony would soon be able to use his veterinary skills on the Quepe farm, but this was only to happen several years later. Then suddenly, on New Year's Eve we were told that we were to be taken to Chol Chol to commence what was to be our ministry there for the next four years.

CHAPTER SIX

A cowboy village

ON A sunny afternoon on New Year's Eve (1952) the mission superintendent drove us in his old Ford T over the hills and across the plain into Chol Chol. We rounded the corner and turned into the dusty road that led to our school compound where we would be living for the next four years. As we did so, I felt our seven year old, Terry, stiffen with suppressed excitement. He was staring goggle-eyed at the tall stockade that bordered our new house and school. Enclosing an area of 100 meters by 100 meters and standing a good 7 feet high, it looked just like the palisade from some thrilling American Wild West film. 'Mum!' he gasped, 'Is that to protect us from the Indians?' Obviously he had visions

of being surrounded by hordes of savages brandishing tomahawks and baying for our blood.

He was right to some extent; Chol Chol did look just like a sleepy little cowboy village. Most of the people lived in modest two-roomed wooden bungalows. The four main streets were dusty tracks in the summer and mud swamps in the winter. During the rainy months the only means of communication with the nearest town was by horse or oxcart.

Chol Chol's mixed population of some 750 inhabitants – the Chileans of Spanish extraction and the Mapuches – were mostly self-supporting, working their own plots of land. Others were employed at one of the flourmills, general stores, or 'drink shops'.

All down our street were tethering posts over which visiting horsemen had thrown their reins. They were especially congregated in front of our cottage hospital and a little further down the street outside the cantina (drink shop). There was a curious connection here. Sadly these cantinas provided a large proportion of our hospital's patients, suffering from injuries ranging from black eyes to knife wounds and broken bones, all caused in drunken brawls.

Most of the day, youths would congregate on the street corner outside our house. Others, I think from a local football club, used to play each evening on the pitch behind our school. As Tony had, like my Dad, been quite hot stuff at soccer in his youth, he thought that this might serve as a good contact point. Accordingly, he went out to join the lads in their game. Their initial reaction was one of muted suspicion. However, to try him out, they passed him the ball shouting, 'Eh! Pastor, you have a go!' Tony hit it on the volley and whacked it into the goal. Grudgingly impressed, they returned it in the air. This time he headed it into the opposite corner. By now their suspicion was beginning to melt into reluctant admiration. So, one of them asked jokingly, 'Pastor! You must have played with Robledo'. Jorge Robledo was the world-famous Chilean player who had scored the winning goal for Newcastle in the previous year's

English Cup Final. Tony, who still didn't speak much Spanish, and understood even less, thought they had said 'Have you heard of Robledo?' and so, wishing to impress, replied 'Si, si' (Yes, yes). Little did he envisage the strange series of events that would unfold as a result of his mistake.

The following week an impressive posse of horsemen, representing a major football club in the nearest big town, rode into Chol Chol with a wad of papers, keen to sign him on for their team. Tony, still not understanding what was going on, refused, but on the grounds that he was busy on Sundays and therefore wouldn't be able to play for them. In spite of this, the legend still persisted in Chol Chol that a top professional soccer star was now residing in their midst.

The real reason for this confusion only came to light some years later when a local Chol Chol team refused to let Tony play against them in a benefit match on the grounds that the rules did not allow professionals to participate. Tony retorted, 'But I've never been a professional'. To this they replied, 'But you must have been, if you played with Robledo'. And then the penny dropped. How easily big misunderstandings can arise from the smallest breakdowns in communications.

I hadn't really given much consideration to the kind of home that we might have. If anything, I suppose I had thought it would be a small, one-floored house built of wood, rather like most of those we had seen on entering the village. In the event, once we had driven through the big double gates of the stockade and we had got out of the car in the school playground, I had time to take in the size of the building. It was huge, with two storeys but made of wood. At first I was quite overawed. However, our part of the building proved to be quite modest – downstairs we had a kitchen and living room, upstairs a bathroom and three bedrooms. The day and boarding schools took up the rest of the building.

As the school term had not yet commenced, the British members of our staff welcomed us warmly into our new home.

These were three single ladies, the Señoritas as they were respectfully called – Miss Maud Bedwell. Miss Muriel Parrott and Miss Doris Tobias. They were eager to offer assistance by lending us anything that we lacked or had not yet unpacked. For me, it was wonderful to be settled at last, especially as the children had adapted so well to their new situation. The fourth member of our team, Miss Royce, was still on home leave in England and would only be returning the following month.

The dirt road in front of the school was about fifty metres wide and ran the whole length of the village. To the right it passed the hospital in the next block, followed by a row of houses. In front of us, and right in the middle of the road, were four enormous Mimosa trees which gave the most gorgeous display of golden blossom at the end of each winter.

Along with the horses tethered in the street outside, there were always a number of ox-carts. Each day, these came rumbling into town from the surrounding countryside. They would offer produce to last us through the winter months, such as sacks of beans, lentils, huge pumpkins, old petrol cans full of honey or lard. Also bundles of dried seaweed, the tubular kind, that we often added to the bean or lentil soups, along with tasty chunks of pumpkin. In winter, these legume soups became our staple diet, and very healthy they were too, providing us with an abundance of protein.

Of course, we had no refrigerator in those days, so I was especially grateful for the honey that allowed me to give the children a special treat throughout the long winter months. The Chileans were, and still are, enthusiastic beekeepers. Our introduction to this was actually quite traumatic. One day we heard a terrific banging of tins in the street and couldn't imagine what was happening. It turned out that someone had spotted a swarm of bees. Apparently, the common belief was that if you banged two saucepan lids together hard enough, the din might attract the swarm and provide you with the chance of enticing the queen to settle in or near your hive. Consequently, whenever people spotted a swarm they would all dive into their homes, grab a couple of saucepan lids and run out into the street crashing them together as hard as they could. It really did sound as if all bedlam had been let loose.

Sometimes a horseman would bring more fragile produce such as eggs. These were carefully rolled up in a long strip of cloth and then tied between each egg to protect them from the jarring of the horse ride. When strung around their neck, such strings looked for all the world like a giant necklace.

I particularly enjoyed it when young children came with tiny quantities of produce from their parents' gardens. There would be a little bunch of spinach, parsley, coriander or even of flowers, a bulb of garlic, a lettuce, a few onions or cherries, one or two eggs etc. They would trot off so happily with their few pesos, when I bought something. On other occasions I was asked if I had a little 'Sal Inglesa' to spare. A literal translation of this would be 'English salt'. 'What can be the difference,' I thought 'between English and Chilean salt?' I discovered later that this was their name for Epsom Salts that in those days was used widely as a laxative, and so thereafter I referred them to the hospital.

Nurse Maud sometimes bought eggs for the hospital from a Mapuche lady who came to the door. Once she complained that the eggs were awfully small. To this came back the surprising reply, 'Well, that's how the chicken laid them. It's not my fault'.

Just round the corner there was a general store where in an emergency you could get most things but for a stiff price. The cost of transport from the big towns was considerable. It stocked a motley collection of items, from aspirins to horse shoes, household goods, sandals made out of old motor tyres (these were especially popular with the country Mapuches), ponchos and sombreros.

The post was brought in once a week. It was carried in two large panniers on the back of a mule, the postman riding alongside. There was no house-to-house delivery, each family had to collect their mail from the post office just one block away from us; it was owned by Señorita Nimia, but run by an assistant; Srta Nimia's real job was that of headmistress of the girls' school.

One of Srta Nimia's other roles was that of Director of the 'Dorcas'. This was a group of ladies who met once a week to make clothes. It was held in various homes and I used to attend regularly. We made simple things like shirts, shorts, frocks and overalls. These were given to us cut out and ready to sew. Most did this by hand but some, who had the luxury of an old fashioned sewing machine, would run them up much more quickly. Once finished, each garment was folded and pressed and then made up into parcels with a few basic gifts such a an exercise book, chalks or crayons, soap or some knitted garments. These parcels would then be given out at Christmas time to the families of widows or other needy persons. In this way we hoped to meet some of the needs of those less fortunate than ourselves. In this fellowship we would also discuss those to whom a visit would be appreciated.

Three years later, I was sitting in one of our Dorcas meetings. Our new nurse and midwife, Shirley Goodwin, was also there. She had come out to replace Miss Royce who was retiring. Miss Royce's farewell ceremony had been most moving; in it we recalled all the wonderful years of service she had given in the Chol Chol hospital.

As things turned out we nearly said farewell to our Dorcas as well, but not intentionally. It was an unusually cold day for this time of years, so we were all huddled around a Chilean brasero, trying to keep warm. This was an open metal pan that had red-hot charcoal burning in it; it was the only means of heating that most homes had. It was my turn to give what should have been a short, closing talk. But somehow I just couldn't wind it up. Everyone still looked interested, but I kept going round and round and round…. Suddenly, Shirley leapt up and flung open the window, letting in a draft of fresh air. This revived us. We then realised that we had been slowly poisoned with the deadly carbon monoxide fumes emitted from the brasero. Quite often we heard of folk who had died when they had gone to sleep with a brasero in a confined space, so this was no joke.

But to return to Srta Nimia's post office. This was quite a feature of our village life. For example, on one occasion it became the centre of a mini-crisis of which dear Miss Royce had been the unwitting cause. She had the bright idea of making an appeal to our home support base for used Christmas cards. These, she thought, could be good for giving out as cards of comfort in bereavement or sickness, for birthdays or other celebrations. So an appeal was printed in the SAMS magazine. Then some enterprising person sent it to 'The Lady', a very up-beat magazine with a large circulation. The result was not what she had expected. Week after week the poor post donkey's panniers were weighed down with enormous, heavy parcels, even sacks, full of Christmas cards. I remember one had £10 worth of stamps on it; big money in those days. If all the postage had been given as donations to SAMS it might have kept our work going for a year! The trouble was that we had no means of stopping the flow. However, the Chileans are an ingenious people and not easily beaten; eventually all the cards were put to good use. When we visited the homes it was nice to see their previously rather drab walls now brightly papered with multitudes of Christmas cards that also kept out the draughts. One family had even made a lovely screen of them to divide their single room into sleeping quarters and livingroom.

Srta Nimia's post office was also the scene of another bizarre episode, but I only discovered this quite recently. It all started when some mysterious 'benefactor' in England sent quarterly packets of comics out for Terry – the Lion, Tiger, Eagle and the Beano. Since I felt that all these, except the Beano, would have a negative effect on him, I decided to restrict his reading to the Beano. Thinking back, I believe I was influenced by the all too recent horrors of the Second World War. We had had enough of wars, especially as we had now several German friends in Chile. The rejected comics were full of stories about the English killing

Germans or cowboys slaughtering Indians by which we were now surrounded. I still take the view that such reading for little children can do them harm and that parents should try to protect them from senseless violence and encourage instead wholesome reading, like the Beano!

At first, Terry put up a mild protest but then submitted surprisingly quickly to my ruling. The reason was, I discovered later, that he had already devised a scheme of 'helping me' by collecting the weekly post from the near-by Post Office. The first time, he didn't tell me that the packet had arrived. Instead, he went to a secret hiding place where he could safely devour his stories undisturbed. When the next package arrived, he carefully wrapped up the old ones and then dutifully presented them to me as if they had just arrived. These he opened in my presence and with a saintly expression on his face, took out the Beano and meekly handed over to me the others that he had already read. Delighted at the success of his ruse, he would then slip away to his secret hiding place where he devoured the contents of the latest packet of comics with considerable relish, smug in the knowledge that from now on he would always be one step ahead of me.

The truth has only now come to light some fifty years later when, in Terry's presence, I was commenting on how obedient he always was as a small boy. It was only then that he ruefully confessed all. However, to this day, he still stoutly maintains that this was merely a conflict of values between British ethics and Chilean ingenuity with, in this case, Chile coming out on top.

CHAPTER SEVEN

The four Señoritas

JUST PRIOR to our arrival in Chol Chol, the responsibility for the work had rested on the shoulders of a small but dedicated team of four single ladies, 'The Señoritas'. Of the four, Miss Royce was by far the most senior. She had worked in Chol Chol for as long as most people could remember! Her authority was by now unbounded and even the toughest and most unruly local lads were overawed by her presence. After all, she had brought most of them into the world!

Miss Royce's main seat of action was the cottage hospital, just down the street from where we lived. This was a two storey wooden building similar to ours but with a balcony round the upstairs floor where the patients, especially those with TB, could sit out and enjoy the clean fresh air. On the ground floor was the out-patients' clinic and on the floor above this were the two wards, one for women, the other for men. This became a place where both Tony and I visited the sick, which we did daily when we were in town. We also held short services for the patients in the wards.

Apart from some Chilean girls that Miss Royce was training as nurses, she also had Maud Bedwell and Muriel Parrott. Together they formed an excellent medical team. Maud Bedwell had come out as a typist and secretary, but Miss Royce had trained her to be her second-in-command in the hospital. She was a pillar of stability. Vivacious Muriel Parrott was a young qualified midwife and nurse. She not only helped in the hospital but also did much of the sick visiting in the town and riding on horseback to patients in the surrounding countryside.

The hospital had come a long way in 30 years; it started when a dispensary had been set up in one small room. Miss Royce had taken charge and in about five years she was treating as many as six thousand patients a year as well as visiting the sick in outlying places. When people were very ill, it was impossible to give them the necessary attention in their own homes. They needed to build a small hospital. To begin with, some of the patients were afraid to stay there. One woman left after two days saying that it made her dizzy being in an upstairs room! Little by little the people gained confidence until, at the time we arrived, there were 14 beds and parents would even happily leave their children.

In the early days the infant mortality rate in Chile was one of the highest in the civilised world; it was said that one child in ten died before reaching the age of two. A regular baby clinic was the answer; mothers would even walk in from distant country areas to attend. After Pattie was born, I used to take her; it gave me a good opportunity to chat with the other Mums and exchange experiences. What a joy it was to see some babies, once so thin, gradually become robust and healthy.

Miss Royce was a person of many unexpected talents. For example, at some unknown time in the past she had acquired the skill of woodcarving. She felt that this would be helpful to pass on to some of the older boys; they might find it useful later to augment their wages. So she used to take a class once a week in our school with the fourth year pupils; boys of about fourteen years old. She asked me if I would like to help her; when I accepted, she taught me how to do it.

To the first class she brought cut out pieces of wood to carve, with the designs already drawn on the surface to guide each pupil. She also came armed with a lot of different sized chisels to do the carving. Once this was finished it was only a matter of assembling the pieces. Some made trays, others boxes or letter racks. Once you got the hang of it, it was amazingly easy and interesting to do the carvings and then to assemble the pieces with glue, and the lids of the boxes with little hinges. At the end of term, it was satisfying to see a table full of the finished products done by the pupils. I think some of these were later stained and polished.

Directly opposite the hospital, on the other side of the road, was the girls' boarding school. This was run most efficiently by Doris Tobias. She was a Canadian girl, an extremely accomplished young lady, always impeccably neat, a highly trained secretary and speed typist and a fluent Spanish speaker. Her Canadian support-base gave her a decided advantage over the rest of us who came from war-impoverished England. It provided her with a seemingly inexhaustible supply of goodies, ranging from beautiful clothes and bedding to the most exciting toys. These she gave as presents to our children and to the children in the boarding school. This was her secret power-base which, oscillating between wheedling and threats, she used with deadly precision to get more than her fair share of her own way! Doris' Mapuche girl gymnasts, in their navy bloomers with a large white ribbon bow perched perkily on the right-hand side of their heads, were the pride of the town.

The girls' boarding school had been founded fifty years before we arrived. A grand lady of Miss Royce's ilk, Miss George, had started it in her tiny home in the village; there she built a few bunk beds for the boarders. She too found it difficult to get the girls to come. The fathers would say, 'My son can go to school. He will be much help to me in my dealings with the Chileans. But why should I send my daughter? Her mother can teach her to spin and weave, and also to dye and cook. What more does she want to know?'

By persisting, she eventually had fourteen girls but for three years the conditions were terribly cramped. Then, on her first home leave, generous supporters raised the funds for her to build the lovely girls' boarding school that we had inherited.

The girls' boarding school also served as a stronghold for the

Señoritas and it was to this that they withdrew to relax over dinner after a hard day's work. The evening meal was always most beautifully prepared by their local cook, Julia. It was quite a formal event: they dressed for dinner, the table was correctly laid and they were served by a team of Mapuche girl boarders who did this in exchange for their food, lodging and training in domestic science. Once they graduated from school, many of these girls got good jobs as maids in one of the bigger cities. Later, I too had three excellent girls in succession all of whom did very well in Santiago. On revisiting Chile after our retirement we still were able to visit them, when they spoilt us no end.

For my part, my first domestic test in our new home was to master the art of cooking bread in the wood-burning stove in the kitchen. This was a totally new experience for me. Having such an excellent Chilean cook, none of my lady colleagues had ever done this either, so they couldn't be of much help. Clearly, I had to seek advice elsewhere and so, in spite of the language barrier, I approached some of my Chilean friends. Although experts in bread making themselves, they all proved to be delightfully vague when it came to the quantities of each ingredient. All you need, they assured me, were some salt, yeast and water, then mix them together in a bowl full of flour, knead well and bake until done. My problem was that I had bowls of various sizes and there was no yeast to be found in Chol Chol.

Eventually, I discovered that people used fermented pumpkin instead of yeast. So from then on I kept some of this bubbling away in a jamjar on the kitchen windowsill. As no one seemed able to explain to me in what proportions this was to be used, I was reduced to the time old method of trial and error. My first attempt needed a hammer and chisel and even then was inedible; not even the dog could get his teeth through it. At my next attempt, the dough had risen so much that it started to roll out of the oven the moment I opened the door. This time we did eat it, but only just! However, I felt I was definitely making progress.

Once I got the hang of it the family used to say that my home-made bread was better than that from a baker's shop. However, as there weren't any baker's shops in Chol Chol, it was difficult for them to prove their point.

Terry particularly loved my later efforts of baking. Indeed, he was so keen to try it out the moment it came out of the oven that I had to insist that he stop breaking off a chunk each time, before it came to the table. For a while, he had been very good at obeying this household rule. One day, as I took the bread out of the oven and turned it out of the tin on to the table, I was called to the kitchen door for a moment. When I got back I spotted that a small chunk of my loaf was missing. I called Terry and sternly pointing to the incriminating evidence, I soundly ticked him off. With an aggrieved expression, he denied any implication in the crime. Then, spotting the missing lump of bread still sitting snugly in the corner of the tin, he triumphantly demanded an apology: 'How could I think he would ever do such a thing to me?'

The multiple facets of our team ministry required careful planning. So from the day we arrived, Tony sought to provide this by having a weekly staff meeting with the four Señoritas and me. Being out-numbered five girls to one chap, I thought this was pretty brave of him! He certainly did find it a little daunting, especially as these Señoritas all had very strong personal opinions on every issue. So, to even things up, he enrolled me as his secret agent within the 'enemy' camp. I could then alert him of any potentially tricky matters that were blowing up. With this foreknowledge, he could hopefully defuse the situation before it actually came up at the staff meeting to threaten our fellowship. Happily, this strategy proved moderately successful.

By subterfuges like these, our staff meetings were by and large happy affairs. Only occasionally did we disagree. On one such occasion Tony and I were ticked off by the others for inviting the humble Mapuche country folk into our home for meals. They seemed to think that this might lead to a loss of respect.

Apparently, it had never been done before and they felt it was rather unsuitable. However, we were unrepentant, and continued to withstand all pressure.

When any of the Señoritas disagreed with a decision they would resort to showing their disapproval by a display of bordom. Miss Royce, who was very deaf, had a simpler and more effective solution. She just switched off her hearing aid.

On just such an occasion Doris, the most conservative of our team, threw a very large yawn to drive home her disdain for Tony's point of view. Unhappily for her, this time she overdid it and dislocated her jaw in the process! The first we knew of this was when she delicately covered her mouth with her lace edged handkerchief while emitting a string of unintelligible grunts. When at last she was persuaded to remove the handkerchief, to our consternation it revealed her mouth stuck in a wide open position!

Fortunately, by now Miss Royce was back in Chol Chol. So instinctively, we all turned to her, as senior nurse, to take the situation in hand; but for all her experience, she had never met this particular abnormality before. Nevertheless, she felt sure it would be covered in her nursing books! So we all trooped over to the hospital to allow her to consult with these – but all to no avail! 'Perhaps a sharp tap under the jaw might do the trick' Miss Royce timidly suggested. But even without the gift of speech, Doris was able to convey in no uncertain terms that she DID NOT think this was a good idea!

By now it was getting late and the possibility of poor Doris having to remain in this unhappy state throughout the night seemed to be increasingly likely. But then, on the morrow, she would still have to face a twenty-mile ride on horseback over rough terrain to our nearest doctor in Temuco to have it reduced. This terrifying prospect was altogether too much for her! She made ever more frantic gesticulations. Her muffled grunts sounded like 'ou-n, u-er and u-u'.

Suddenly I thought I understood: could it be 'down, under

and up'? Throwing up a quick prayer and caution to the wind, I inserted my thumbs into Doris' mouth and firmly pushed her lower jaw down, under and up. There was a loud crack and, low and be-hold, the dislocation was reduced – but only on one side! Lop-sided, it now resembled a grotesquely squashed pear!

A little tear trickled down Doris' cheek, so I plucked up all my courage to have yet another attempt. This time, miraculously, the mouth was restored to its true proportions. Needless to say, from then on a very chastened Doris was a little more circumspect about demonstrating her boredom in Tony's staff meetings!

CHAPTER EIGHT

Living on a shoe-string

MATTHEW WAS the most placid of the mission horses, ideal for young or inexperienced riders. When he was available, Tony would sometimes ask Terry, now just turned eight years old, if he would like to ride with him to one of the nearer rural schools. On just such an occasion, as they were sloshing through the mud, Tony and his companion, Don Germán (pronounced 'Hair mán), got out ahead. Eventually, on looking back, Tony saw his young son struggling vigorously to counteract Matthew's lethargy. In his desperation he had actually turned round in the saddle to face the tail where he was walloping Matthew's flanks for all his worth with a small switch, but all to no avail. Eventually they did reach their destination, but with a very disgruntled Terry.

The return journey did much to restore his good spirits. Here, they came across a tiny maiden in distress. A little Mapuche girl had got hopelessly stuck in the deep mud. The more she tugged the deeper she sunk. At this, every ounce of chivalry in his body welled up within Terry's young breast. Leaping from the saddle, he struggled over to where the maiden was entrenched and between them they managed to clamber out to higher and drier ground. Great was Terry's glee as, on returning home, he recounted to me at length every detail of his act of gallantry. He felt that this was a typical case of the priest (Dad) and the Levite (Don Germán) passing by on the other side, leaving him, the Good Samaritan, to do all the dirty work. Whatever! It had certainly done wonders for Terry's self-esteem!

As I too was new to riding, whenever I was invited to go out with Miss Royce, I was also given Matthew. Terry's poison was my meat! On one such occasion, we set off on a lovely summer's day. I remember how the gorse seed-pods kept popping in the intense heat. Miss Royce looked very regal, riding side-saddle, as she always did, and wearing a long brown skirt and gloves.

On arrival, she held a simple service in the school. As we said goodbye, and remounted, a hen with her brood of tiny yellow chicks shot out from the entrance of the ruca right under Matthew's hooves. A ruca is a Mapuche straw hut. Totally out of character, because he was so frightened by the chicks Matthew reared up and sat back heavily on the ruca. There was an ominous crunch of tearing straw and branches and cries of alarm from the panic-stricken occupants. A startled Miss Royce gasped weakly, 'Oh! My dear! You've gone quite white.' Later I discovered that at the time I was expecting our next baby, Pattie, so perhaps this

was the reason.

As Matthew quickly regained his composure, I was able to remain mounted. The Chilean saddles, unlike Tony's English one, rise steeply both in front and behind. So, as I was firmly wedged in, this must have helped to save me.

On the return journey, Matthew was completely back to his old self as he placidly dawdled along. Consequently, Miss Royce began to leave me behind. Suddenly I found that the bridle was hanging limply in my hand. The string with which it had been repaired had broken and the bit had come out of Matthew's mouth leaving me with no control over him. Because Matthew was placid I came to no harm and was able to dismount and mend it.

So, whether the bridle had been repaired with a shoe-string or just any other odd piece of string, we certainly had to run our station on a 'shoe-string'. Apparently, there was no money to pay Chol Chol's first quarter's station allowance. Tony would have to make do with the tiny balance in hand that he had inherited from the previous quarter.

In no way would the money received cover even half our projected expenses. We really did have to look to God to come to our rescue. He did, but in the most unexpected way. We suddenly received a personal gift of £80.00, known as a 'Couty Grant'. This was about a quarter of our year's wages. Then the partners in our old practise in Ilfracombe decided to set aside 10% of each year's profit, as a donation to our work. We were able to use these extra sums to cover the most pressing expenses of the Mission hoping that perhaps, if better days dawned, we could one-day pay ourselves back our special Couty grant.

Obviously, the cost of running such a large station was considerable. In summer we had to pay for the horses grazing rights and then buy in sacks of oats for the winter. The horses also had to be shod and all the harnesses and saddles repaired. There were the 'Gratifications' to pay. These were small incentives given yearly to each rural teacher for his services. Their real pay came

from the government in the form of 'Subventions', but these were running late, on this occasion two years in arrears. So, along with any animals or cash-crops they could sell, the 'Gratificacions' came as a great help in tiding them over.

Perhaps our largest expense was the purchase of a huge quantity of wood to fuel the stoves in the houses and hospital. From the end of July to the beginning of October each year, this wood came down the river. Tree trunks, felled high up in the hills, were bound firmly together to make large rafts and floated down the river for sale along the way. The owner would stand on his raft and steer it perilously with a long pole; it was their version of a punt out for a lazy day on the river Cam.

Obviously this was a time consuming occupation, especially as one never knew when they would arrive. Then Tony had to haggle over the price of every raft. This year the price ranged from over 100 pesos per trunk for the first rafts, to 20 pesos for the last. As someone had told him that the price had been 5 pesos per trunk at the end of the previous year, he felt he was being taken for a bit of a ride, and refused to buy at a 100. This strategy paid off, and eventually he bought over 700 trunks at an average of 30 pesos. On our budget this was still big money.

Once each raft had been purchased, he still had the job of employing someone with oxen to haul the trunks out of the river and then, one by one, the four hundred meters up to the Mission. Then came fresh haggling over price, usually another 6 pesos per trunk. All this was most distasteful to Tony, but an essential duty if we were to survive the year financially.

Finally, we had to contact Bill Flagg to ask for the tractor and circular saw from Quepe. We were tremendously grateful when six men turned up to cut the logs and another three to paint the church. None of them had beds and so it fell to my lot to rig them up with something. The woodcutters could only stop four days, so after discussion they agreed to work over-time. Tony then wrote to Bill to ask him to add this to their wages when they got back. The other three stayed on a month and made a wonderful job of painting our Chol Chol church.

Once again we had much cause to be thankful. None of these things would have been possible but for the miraculous provision of the Couty Grant and the generous donation from our veterinary colleagues in England. Yes, we were beginning to repair the mission property, even if it was on a shoestring.

From our earliest days we had been surprised at how many visitors came from near and far to such a remote place. Of course, this was only in the summer when the roads were open for lorries and cars. In the winter, access was limited to horse or ox cart that had to plough through deep mud.

Some of these visitors returned to their base to raise support for the mission. This also helped us to survive our serious financial crisis. Among the earliest of these visitors was our immediate predecessor, Peter Tadman and his wife Elsie. From Chol Chol, he had moved on to Concepción on the Pacific coast. They were to help us in so many ways.

For example, very soon after their first visit, our family fell seriously ill with hepatitis. For three weeks, Tony and I could hardly keep anything down, the vomiting was so severe. I will describe this in more detail in a later chapter entitled 'In sickness and in health'. When our friends heard of out situation, they immediately invited us to Concepción to convalesce.

If we could get to the train in Temuco they said they would meet us at the other end. This was daunting enough, as to get to Temuco we would have to ride on the back of the local storekeeper's lorry. However, it was well worth it – we spent a wonderful week resting and being able to eat and drink suitable food, such as fruit and fish; things that were not available in Chol Chol in winter.

That evening Peter took us to get our first glimpse of the Pacific Ocean. On the coast, it was so bracing that it did us a world of good. The sunset was fantastic. It was also encouraging to find that Peter and Elsie had created quite considerable interest among the English community in Miss Royce's hospital. They sent us back with a supply of medicines as a donation. The days of rest slipped by far too quickly. On the lorry journey back to Chol Chol, Tony managed to get the two little girls and me into the cabin. As usual, he and Terry had to ride on the open back where it was bitterly cold and crowded.

Our meeting with the Tadmans was one of an extraordinary chain of events stretching from Tony's school days and right up to the present time. We only discovered the first link in this chain by chance, when Tony happened to mention how, years before, his father had brought a scratch cricket eleven to play his school team. The captain of this scratch eleven had been a certain Mr. Tadman. To our amazement he turned out to be Peter's Dad!

But the chain of events continued when they told us that their son, Philip, had been born in Chol Chol hospital during the time that they had been living there. Years later, when Philip Tadman had grown up, he returned to Chol Chol to show his children where he had been born. Sadly, by that time, the hospital had been burnt down and so all they could see was a large, empty field. Afterwards, his little son was overheard telling someone enthusiastically, 'I saw the field where my Daddy was born!'

It was Peter who first introduced us to Ian Morrison, then a bank clerk in Concepción. He was the grandson of 'Daddy' Wilson, the founder of our Chol Chol mission. Sometime later Ian was the first resident when we opened a student hostel in Temuco. He had, of course, been born in Chile, and eventually became our first national bishop in the Republic.

This chain has now extended to the third generation. For many years, Phil Tadman, Peter's son, has been the treasurer of SAMS. So this remarkable chain now spans over seventy years, from the friendship on the cricket pitch of Tony's father with Peter's father and right up to the present day. This is just another example of how tiny seeds planted so long ago have produced such a useful harvest today. It has given us a wonderful insight into God's faithfulness to us over all these years.

CHAPTER NINE

Fiestas and the Chilean school year

WITH THE start of each new school year, our little cowboy village suddenly rubbed its sleepy eyes and woke up. Hundreds of eager children came crowding into our previously deserted school playground and school building. All was now bustle and activity.

Only Terry was of school age, but Rosemary and Hilary used to sit in unofficially in the primary class. The teachers and children both made them very welcome and, of course, their Spanish improved in leaps and bounds as a result.

On Rosemary's birthday, all day long a stream of her school friends brought her little gifts such as a hair slide, a ribbon or an egg, a peacock feather, flowers or sweets. This, in spite of the fact that they had only known her for two days, when the school year had reopened.

Although the winters were bitterly cold, there was no heating in the classrooms. To keep their hands warm, the children would bring stones to school that they had previously heated at home by putting them in the embers of the fire or an oven. These they put in their pockets where they could clutch them for warmth during class time. However, as the morning drew on, they would gradually cool down. So, in 'recreo' (break for recreation) little groups of twos and threes would come shyly up to the kitchen door to ask if I would reheat them in my wood oven. I so much enjoyed getting to know them in this way.

I discovered that the school had another use for stones when one night, with Tony in church, I was sitting alone by the fire at home. Suddenly I heard the queerest rattling noises coming from one of the primary school classrooms. With my heart pounding and grasping my precious torch, I crept up thinking someone had broken in. I flung open the door only to see a number of rats scuttling and stones that they were playing with scattering in every direction. These stones were the ones the little children used for maths, such as counting etc.

For Tony, there were now the daily assemblies to attend to and we both had English classes to take and all the boarders to look after. True, there was a housemaster whose task it was to care for the boy boarders, but Tony had to share some of that responsibility. For my part, I also had another mouth to feed as Don Germán the housemaster now began to board with us. But most of all, there were the fiestas to enjoy, dotted through the year, like stars shining in an otherwise dreary sky. At the centre of these was always the Chilean flag.

The Chileans were rightly proud of their flag. Anything that to them could be construed as disrespectful to it would be fiercely resented. Their patriotic fervour for the flag became even more intense on national fiestas or feast days, when they celebrate the great events from their history. On these occasions, the school always ran a show or 'programa'. Selected scholars, teachers and other volunteers would put on their respective acts, often brilliantly. One of our lady missionaries who was never slow to take part in such events, decided to co-operate. Suddenly, to the dismay of all, she, a foreigner, came prancing on the stage with her body totally wrapped in the Chilean flag. A full-scale riot was about to break out. Only the speedy intervention of the headmaster saved her from a possible untimely death by lynching!

21st May, the ' Día de Arturo Prat' (Arturo Prat's Day) was the first of the yearly patriotic feasts to be celebrated in Chol Chol. In the war of the Pacific, Arturo Prat was a captain in the Chilean navy in charge of two small ships, with the order to blockade the port of Iquique. They were confronted with two major iron-clads that the enemy, Peru, had recently purchased from Britain. Arturo's ship, the Esmeralda, was a wooden vessel captured from the Spanish decades before. Also it was hopelessly outgunned. However, rather than pull down the Chilean flag and surrender, they all continued fighting to the end.

One of the Peruvian iron-clads, the Huascar, eventually rammed Arturo's wooden vessel to sink her. Prat leapt aboard the enemy ship, armed only with a cutlass and pistol, in a brave attempt to capture the vessel, but was immediately mowed down by his opponents. Meanwhile, the sinking Esmeralda was slipping under the waves, its unsurrendered Chilean flag still flying proudly from her mast. As a last act of defiance, the doomed crew fired a single salvo from her one remaining canon. It now became a matter of national pride for the Chilean navy to avenge the death of Prat and the loss of the Esmeralda. Their whole fleet was sent to hunt down the Huascar and later that same year they captured and triumphantly integrated her into the Chilean navy. All this was taught with passion to the children in every Chilean school. It had a profound effect upon our Terry. When listening to a radio play about this event, he sat transfixed, with tears streaming down his face.

On Arturo Prat Day the whole town turned out in celebration. Our school children paraded in force, marching through the town and ending up at the carabineros' headquarters. The carabineros make up the renowned Chilean police force that plays such a major roll in keeping law and order. Their name comes from Carbine, or light rifle, because on high days they carry rifles (and ceremonial swords) which certainly lends a special air of authority to their operations. For their day-to-day duties, they wear a loaded revolver slung on their belt which to us, accustomed to the ordinary English Bobby, gave them a slightly threatening appearance.

Our school parade (desfile) was quite impressive. To start with, it was very long, composed of over two hundred children, all dressed impeccably in their white starched 'delantales' (smocks). These were worn in order that all children, rich or poor, Chilean or Mapuche, would be dressed in exactly the same way, making 'the have nots' indistinguishable from the 'haves'.

The 'desfile' was led by our excellent school drum and pipe band. I doubt if there were many other towns of our size that could come up with anything as good. It took some time to march all round the town and then almost as much again to assemble in formation outside the carabineros' headquarters. By now there was an air of high expectation among the crowd that had gathered to watch.

The heart of the ceremony was, of course, to honour the memory of Arturo Prat and his great acts of bravery. During the hoisting of the flag, one of our schoolboys, especially chosen on merit for his oratorical skills, was to recite a poem extolling these acts of bravery.

To initiate the proceedings, one of the three carabineros marched smartly out and grasped the cord of the flag. As he did so the others snapped to attention and held their prolonged salute impeccably. Then to our horror, disaster struck; the flag just wouldn't hoist. However hard the poor carabinero pulled, it just stubbornly refused to budge. By now the poem had reached its dramatic conclusion with a description of the Esmeralda's flag, eternally flying at the top of its mast never to be lowered. It seemed sadly incongruous, therefore, that in fact it was still lying limply on the bottom of its mast. Sensing that all was not well, the unfortunate orator ground to a halt and the salute to the flag that wasn't also came to an abrupt end. Then, just as this happened, the cord must have freed itself, because now, too late, the flag simply hurtled to the top of its mast. A very embarrassed policeman beamed with relief. After all – 'better late than never'.

Another prominent feature of the celebrations was an old canon that was made to fire one lone shot at the precise hour as that of the last canon-shot of the sinking Esmeralda. When Terry was ten, he decided to mount his own private salute to his hero, Arturo Prat. So on one quiet morning, the peace of Chol Chol was disturbed by a bang, as Terry came bounding into the house beside himself with glee. 'Come, come and see' he said 'Come and look at the canon I've made.' I must say it looked quite impressive. It was a large water-pipe, cemented in at one end and bound by wire to a huge wooden block. It was Terry's replica of one he had seen in the Eagle comic, modelled on a canon from an old man o' war.

'Let me fire it for you again' he pleaded. But to Terry's disgust, Tony sternly intervened with a 'No way, it would be far too dangerous.' 'But Dad,' wheedled Terry 'just once more, pleeease, At least let me use up my last little bit of gunpowder'. So Tony reluctantly relented. 'Well, all right. But do it in the middle of the school playground, give it a really long fuse and then get right out of the way' he consented. What he hadn't realised was that Terry's 'little' was in fact the best part of a quarter of a kilo (half a pound). It was this amount of gunpowder that he now proceeded to pack into the barrel.

At last the scene was set and the canon duly mounted in the centre of the 100 by 100 meter school playground. Terry then withdrew to watch patiently as his long fuse gradually burnt through. What happened next was the utterly unexpected, the like of which we never wish to hear again. An ear shattering blast brought Chol Chol to a frozen standstill, while all that remained of the canon was a hole in the ground and a board from the palisade, some 50 meters away, flapping idly in the breeze where the barrel of the canon had just passed through. But a wide-eyed Terry had entered into the annals of Chol Chol's history books. Such was the nature of our sleepy little cowboy village at that time that a young school boy could buy any quantity of gunpowder over the counter of a local store.

This episode took us back to an incident that occurred while we were still in Ilfracombe. Terry was four at the time and he had a habit, when he had his prayers at night, of carrying on a dialogue with God about the day's affairs. Having told God about something he'd been doing, he would then give me God's reply

from out of the side of his mouth. One night, when he had been disobedient, I started by saying, 'You've told me you're sorry, now ask God to make you a good boy. Quickly he said, 'Please God, make me a good boy'. God's response came loud and clear, out of the side of his mouth, 'He says he won't'. After the canon episode, we were now beginning to wonder if in fact Terry hadn't been right all the time. Perhaps God hadn't! No, not really.

The second and perhaps the most important of the national fiestas was 'dieciocho'. This commemorates the independence of Chile from Spanish rule on the 18th of September, 1810. Anyone who has attended these celebrations will never forget the excitement of making, and eating, the wonderful little fried pasties called empanadas.

As usual, our school was very much on parade. On this particular dieciocho, Rosemary was now a pupil, as well as Terry. Hilary was still enjoying her unofficial status, which just suited her placid disposition. She was quite content to follow and copy the other children, so I made her a white delantal (pinafore) like them and provided her with her own minute Chilean flag on a stick for her to wave. She really did look cute, with her two little pigtails, tied up with white bows to match her delantal. When the real day dawned, there she was, appearing from nowhere, just in time to float into position as they all formed up in the large school playground.

Sharp on the appointed hour, off they went, led by the band in which her big brother, Terry, was now the proud drum major. After the usual long march round the town they arrived outside the carabineros' headquarters where the mayor and all his dignitaries were assembled. In perfect formation they marked time, until the command came 'Halt!' when everyone snapped to attention. Everyone, that is, except for one diminutive figure right at the very end of the rank. Hilary just kept on going with her marking time, completely in a world of her own, but still clutching her little flag. There was a roar of laughter that quickly turned into a great cheer of approval. Even a row of nuns, not noted in those days for their exuberance, joined in the cheers.

But throughout, Hilary, in a world of her own, remained totally oblivious to the enthusiasm she was creating among her huge crowd of admiring fans.

The third national fiesta celebrated as part of our school year was on the 12th October; it was called the 'Día de la Raza'. In this, the Chileans remember when Christopher Columbus first landed on Hispañola. On one such Día de la Raza we all went down to the football ground. On arrival, we found that the Mapuches were engaged in a fierce game of Chueca, their equivalent to our hockey, played with sticks and a wooden ball wrapped in leather. The two teams lined up parallel to the sidelines, each player facing one of his opponents. The pitch was so narrow that the sticks of the opponents clashed with each other, and often with the person too. To our unpractised eye, it appeared to be a particularly ferocious sport. The idea of the game was to whack the ball as hard as you could towards and over your opponents' goal line. To facilitate this, at each end, in front of their opponents' goal line, a Mapuche witchdoctor (a Machi) was sweeping the ground with a branch from a sacred tree to get rid of any evil spirits that might impede the entry of their own team's ball. According to their belief, the team with the strongest Machi would be the one that scored the most goals.

On our first 12th October in Chile, a good crowd of our

people from the Chol Chol church, as well as many more that had come into town from our rural schools, congregated in the football ground for a united act of witness. I remember this, because on that day I was feeling particularly uncomfortable, as baby was due any time. So I was especially upset when, as Tony was preaching, a drunken horseman galloped furiously up to him, brandishing a knife within a few inches of his face. 'If you don't stop preaching, I'll stab you to death' he roared. Tony held his ground and quietly replied, 'Friend, Jesus loves you and can free you from this vice if you will let him'. For a while the man continued to brandish his knife; then he turned round and with a further oath galloped off. As he did so, a large lump of mud from the horse's hoof struck Tony on the side of the head, sending him reeling. We were all thankful, however, that this was our only casualty!

The next evening the Señoritas invited Tony and me over to dinner. While we were enjoying the meal, a niggling backache began to increase. I thought, 'This may be baby on the way'. I waited until we began to disperse and then said to Muriel, 'I think it would be wise if you came over, prepared to sleep the night our side'. We had been a little anxious because of my serious complications with a partially retained placenta and heavy haemorrhaging, after Hilary's birth in Slough. Although we had complete confidence in Muriel's skill, we were obviously only too aware that the nearest doctor was a twenty-mile horse ride away in Temuco. However, our prayers were wonderfully answered and everything progressed nicely.

At 6 a.m. the next morning, the 14th of October, 1953, baby Patricia arrived safely, at eight and a half pounds. Tony had helped Muriel throughout and had even given me an injection to ensure the speedy expulsion of the placenta this time. Good old veterinary experience, again! At 6.30 we were joined by a sleepy Terry, Rosemary and Hilary, who all sat mesmerised in a row on the side of the bed, each holding Pattie in turn. Terry had longed for a brother and felt very hopeful this time, so I whispered to him, 'Don't let her see you are disappointed that she is a girl'. With a gulp he said to Pattie, 'I'm glad you are a little girl really'.

Next day, poor Muriel went down with flu'. However, with three extra pairs of willing little hands, plus Tony's, I was able to cope just fine. But, oh my! Were they extravagant with my precious supply of Talcum Power!

CHAPTER TEN

Pots and privies

AS A lad, Tony used to spend all his holidays with his grandparents in Devonshire, in their cottage in Seaton. In those days there was only an outside privy. He always maintains that this was good preparation for the rather more primitive conditions that we would later encounter in South America. In actual fact, in our home in Chol Chol we were relatively well off. Although we were attached to the boy's boarding school dormitory we had a separate bathroom with running water that was pumped up from the river about four hundred metres away. This river water was for washing and bathing only; it was much too dirty to drink. Our crystal clear drinking water was drawn up in a bucket from a deep well in the school playground. We were very satisfied with this until one day, during the routine cleaning of the well, they found the putrid bodies of two chickens and a dead rat at the bottom.

The boarders were Mapuche lads who came in from the surrounding country. Their nominal fees to enter the 'internado' were paid in sacks of wheat and beans at harvest time. The boys' dormitory was a huge, long attic over the classrooms, housing about forty lads. In the corner was a small bedroom where Don Germán, the housemaster, slept. There was also a connecting door between the dormitory and our part of the building. The boys slept on wooden frames, each softened by sheepskins which served as mattresses. This arrangement was particularly suited for the fleas. During term time they would opt for the larger and more succulent pastures in the dormitory. It was only when the

70

lads went home for their school holidays that hordes of fleas, cheated of their normal fare, marched under the connecting door into our corridor and bedrooms, demanding redress. When we discovered the cause of our sudden discomfort we naturally took defensive action. As they seemed to be impervious to DDT, we eventually resorted to the more basic but effective technique of torch and damp soap. Diving under the bedclothes, one would hold the torch while the other enveloped the culprits one by one in the soggy end of the tablet.

The boarders were not so well served as we were for toilets. They had to use the school latrine in the playground; this resembled somewhat the system Tony had known in Seaton many years before. It was comprised of a large privy shed perched on boards over a deep pit. One morning Don Germán had been moving the old privy shed and putting it over a new one, with a gang of pupils as his helpers. The old exposed pit was now full and had therefore been put strictly out of bounds until it could be filled up with earth.

I remember this because there had been a series of petty thefts at the time; for several nights clothes had been missing from the boys' dormitory. Don Germán, convinced that the culprit was breaking in from outside, had set a rota of boarders to watch throughout the night. Sure enough, one of the guards surprised the thief and rousing the dormitory they all set off in hot pursuit across the school playground, splitting the silence with the most blood-curdling war cries. Don Germán brought up the rear, brandishing his revolver and firing warning shots excitedly into the air. From our bedroom window we had a grandstand view of the whole scene.

In the bright moonlight we could see the thief making for the nearest boundary fence. The pursuers, of course, had the advantage over him with their inside knowledge. With a cynical disregard for their teacher's ban, we realised that they were heading the thief off towards the area that had been put out of bounds that morning.

Their ruse was cruelly successful. With a cry of horror the unfortunate victim suddenly found himself suspended in mid-air, his flailing legs continuing their frantic revolutions, I suppose through sheer force of habit, as there was now no solid support to justify this. For a moment he seemed to hang there; then, with a succulent splosh, he plunged into the foetid trap, the gaping latrine pit they had exposed that morning. The vengeful horde surged round him just as his head and shoulders appeared over the ledge in a desperate attempt to scramble out. To our consternation they shoved him down again. Finally, to our relief, Don Germán puffed up and justice was at last tempered by mercy.

During the daytime the boarders used these latrines, but at night their facilities were reduced to one large bucket in the middle of the floor. We became acutely aware of this in a rather unusual way – it was due to the rats. I couldn't understand why the soap kept disappearing from the bathroom and thought somebody must be taking it. On hearing a thud one night I crept in with a torch and found the soap had been knocked off the ledge and propelled towards a rat hole. A feature of the house to which we found particular difficulty in adjusting during our early days was the sound of these rats scrambling around between the inner and outer skirting of the wooden walls, squealing and fighting as they went.

One night we were wakened by howls of agony coming from the boys' dormitory. In trying to get to a piece of bread that a lad had smuggled under his pillow, a rat had mistaken his ear for the bread. Frightened by the hullabaloo, the rat clung on for grim death while the unfortunate boy, screaming with pain, raced around the dormitory trying to shake it off.

Another night we were again wakened by howls, but this time of triumph rather than of agony. The borders had been losing things from their store of tuck and, suspecting the rats, had decided to lay a trap for them. A short board was balanced over the side of the communal slop-bucket in the middle of the floor and a lump of soap temptingly placed on the inner end. Lured by the bait, a rat had literally 'walked the plank', and tipped to its doom in the bucket. With whoops of delight the boys swooped on their quarry.

When the boys and Don Germán left the internado during the school holidays the wooden buildings seemed huge and empty. On nights when Tony also had to be away visiting the country people, Don Germán insisted on leaving his revolver with me. I was far more afraid of this than of any potential burglar and so stowed it away on the top of the wardrobe, as far out of reach of the children as possible. One time in the dead of night I heard the strangest shuffling noises under my bedroom window. Groping around for something suitable to drop on the intruder I lighted on an old flowered chamber pot inherited from some previous occupant. Creeping to the window with this weapon I was relieved to find that it was only one of our horses that had broken loose from its tether. I crawled sheepishly back into bed only glad that I discovered the identity of the intruder before releasing my heavy missile.

Our experiences of pots and privies in Chile certainly prepared us for even more primitive conditions in Paraguay and Argentina. In Paraguay for example, there where all kinds of poisonous creatures skulking around the latrines so we used to drop burning newspaper down the hole first, to drive out any hidden hornet or snake. On one occasion Terry was occupied in one of these outside privies when he suddenly spotted two evil-looking hornets eyeing him malevolently. Seriously outnumbered, two to one, he decided to leg it. As the creatures made a dive for him, he reached the door in the nick of time but pant-less. In spite of Terry's undoubted agility, his assailants set off in hot pursuit determined to press home their advantage. They were clearly now in no mood for taking prisoners but with deadly accuracy both hit their target – right on that part of his anatomy which had been so temptingly over-exposed to their evil designs.

But there was another toilet in Paraguay that we especially looked forward to revisiting! Its walls were adorned by a colony of tiny yellow frogs. These had suckers on their feet, which allowed them to cling around the walls in the quaintest postures. These little fellows panted, as if permanently out of breath, their tummies going in and out like a pair of bellows. They were so cute that one could watch enthralled, quite oblivious to the queue of postulants outside, all desperately jogging on the spot!

The Wichi also had trouble with their toilet facilities; they are one of the indigenous tribes that inhabit the Argentine Chaco. Most of them are settled in villages of straw huts between the Bermejo and the Pilcomayo rivers. From Paraguay Tony often visited them. The Chaco is dusty, scrub land; about the only vegetation which grows in the natural state is the gnarled Algarroba tree. Yet under the guidance of our agriculturists this semi-desert, when irrigated, was beginning to blossom like the rose. Gradually the Wichi began to clear the scrub and to replace it with crops of sweet peppers, tomatoes and the like. These were sent by steam train to the capital, Buenos Aires, where they were marketed.

After a while the missionaries noted a marked rise in the number of bicycles among the Wichi; indeed, every family now seemed to possess one. For a while they were mystified. Granted, with their new cash crops, the people were better off, but why this extraordinary obsession with bicycles? At last, when questioned, one of the Wichi patiently explained: 'Well! How else do you expect us to get to the toilet, now it's so far away?' Then the truth dawned. Their toilet was the bush that previously had been just outside their back doors. As more and more land had been cleared, their 'toilet' had receded into the distance. Thus their need for modern transport to 'go to the toilet'. In other words, if you cut back the scrub that such communities use as their toilets, it is not sufficient just to teach them how to irrigate and cultivate the land; you must also teach them how to construct latrines. How easily such a finely tuned ecological balance can be disturbed if there is insufficient understanding of the local culture.

It is equally dangerous to provide improved toilet facilities without carefully teaching how these are to be used. Things that we take for granted in our culture may be quite foreign to another. On his first visit to a modern city, one of our Wichi friends got caught this way. On being asked if he wanted to wash his hands, he was shown into the loo. Seeing the sparkling, clean water in the lavatory pan he naturally proceeded to wash his hands and face in it. When his host discovered what had happened he derided the stupidity of the 'ignorant Indian'. He would have been better employed giving him a friendly word of explanation as to its more traditional use. So many wars have been caused by leaders misunderstanding each other's cultures that it's surely our duty to take the trouble to understand the customs of others rather than to condemn them out of hand. In this respect, it is encouraging that we can draw such important cultural and sociological lessons even from such an unlikely subject as 'Pots and Privies'!

CHAPTER ELEVEN

Off the mark!

ONE OF the first patients we visited in the hospital was a Mapuche named Arturo Coñuepan. He and his brother had been pupils in our Chol Chol school. After moving to Santiago, his brother had eventually become Minister for Agriculture. This was an extraordinary achievement for a Mapuche Indian and it reflected something of the esteem in which our school was held in some government circles. We wanted to build upon this foundation laid down by our predecessors.

To identify more closely with these down-trodden people, Tony started to learn their native language, Mapudungun ('The Word of the Land'). By law, all our schools had to teach in Spanish so most of the men, and quite a few of the younger women, spoke this (for them) second language fairly well. There were still a number of the older women, however, who could only speak Mapudungun. Thus Tony's desire to be able to say a few simple words to them in their own language.

To encourage the Mapuches to set up rural schools staffed with their own people, the Ministry of Education had originally been willing to recognise teachers with only three years of primary education. Using this early government concession, our founding missionaries had established a school, up to 3rd year primary, in each of about twenty surrounding Mapuche communities.

During the war years these rural schools had run down. On the other hand, the Chilean system of education was moving on fast and so our schools were being left behind. Correctly, they were beginning to insist on at least six years of primary schooling. We could see that soon the level would be raised to 3rd year 'humanidades' (secondary education), and so on. Clearly, as higher standards were being required, we had to act quickly if we were to avoid the gradual closure of all our country schools for lack of teachers with the necessary qualifications.

We felt that it was worth fighting for these rural schools. They had not only provided excellent education for many country children but had also served as centres for our medical outreach and in most cases for simple Sunday services. We found that most of these services had been discontinued, so, in our weekly staff meeting, we all agreed that we would try to encourage the teachers to recommence them to restore a spiritual dimension to the academic one.

Over time the indigenous people had learnt to rely on us to represent their interests before the authorities. Eventually they were even willing to entrust their girls, as well as their boys, to our boarding establishments where they could continue their education up to 6th year primary.

But now our Mapuche children from Chol Chol school needed further secondary education, especially if they wanted to become teachers in one of our schools. At that time, we hadn't sufficient qualified teachers to start our own Liceo (secondary school) in Chol Chol. The only option seemed to be to open a youth hostel in Temuco so that the Mapuche children could then study in one of the State Liceos there. Thus our longing for Doug and Ros Milmine to join us with a view that one day they would be able to establish such a centre in Temuco.

It was at this time that I received a letter from Ros Milmine herself to say that their fifth child, baby Stephen, had been born. Unable to keep the good news to myself, I ran along to share it with Maud at the hospital. On getting back, Tony had to break the terrible news from a second letter from the same post bag which told how Stephen had been a blue baby and had died only two days later. This came as an awful shock, especially so soon after the first good news. We grieved together with our dear friends in their loss.

We couldn't help wondering if this tragedy would affect their plans to join us in Chile. However, by the grace of God our misgivings turned out to be unfounded. After consultations with the committee, they were accepted and to our great joy, arrived in Quepe on the 12th Feb, 1954. There they set up home in the bungalow just across the orchard from the quaint little church.

One of the first events that Doug and Ros organised in Quepe was the marriage of our dear friend Bill Flagg to his fiancée Marjorie. She had come out from England after a separation of over two years. On May 4th 1954 they were at last married in Quepe church among a large group of their rejoicing friends.

Our party got there the night before after a truly awful journey to Temuco on the tractor and trailer. The road was full of potholes, and the trailer felt as if it had no springs. Consequently I had a tricky job trying to breast-feed Pattie. With each bump and jerk, she lost hold, so in the end I had to give up to which her protest was loud and long. Only when we reached Temuco was I able to change and feed her. I'd learnt my lesson and shamelessly I did what I'd always said I would never do – I went to the shop over the road, and bought her a dummy. So on the trailer, for the second leg of the journey from Temuco to Quepe, she slept happily, dummy in mouth, although it was equally bumpy.

On arrival, Tony accompanied Bill, the bridegroom, to a neighbour's house, Rodney Hemans, where they slept the night. The girls and I stayed with the bride at the Milmines. Here we helped to prepare the food for the huge crowd that we expected on the morrow. While Ros baked a beautiful wedding cake, I ironed Marjorie's frilly wedding dress. This she had packed away two years previously patiently waiting for this day. It was therefore something of a job to iron. Eventually, we all fell into bed about 2 a.m. totally exhausted. It had certainly been some day! It had been so busy that apparently poor Doug had completely forgotten that it was his birthday!

Next day (Woops! No! Sorry, later the same day!) we were up bright and early. It was a lovely morning. Rodney brought over the bridal coach, his trap drawn by two horses, which he had kindly provided. This he had tastefully draped with a white sheet to protect the dresses. Meanwhile, I helped the bridesmaid, a very happy Rosemary, into her simple white frock, and placed two red copihues in her hair. The copihue is the beautiful, waxy, bell-like national flower of Chile and so was particularly appropriate for the occasion.

Marj and our Rosemary looked lovely as they drove through the orchard in the horse-drawn trap to the door of Quepe church. Rodney drove the trap while Doug sat with the girls as he was to give Marj away. The church was packed, with many having to listen from outside. Tony took the bi-lingual service, principally in Spanish, of course, but with concessions in English so that Marj could understand. We were all so happy to see our dear friends start their new life together, that God would so abundantly bless.

After the beautiful ceremony, we all trouped over to the farm where Bill had arranged a mammoth barbecue, in traditional Chilean style, for the farm workers and neighbours, of whom sixty were invited but over a hundred and fifty turned up! But all were well fed.

Just after the Milmine's arrival, our rather conservative superintendent returned to England on home leave. Then we received a letter informing us of his resignation and appointing Tony in his place. At such an early point in our ministry this seemed to be a huge responsibility but, fully supported by Bill Flagg and Doug Milmine, we felt also that it was a great challenge. It certainly now gave us scope to pursue a number of exciting projects that we all felt were necessary. Not least of these was Doug's move into Temuco which, for some reason, the previous superintendent hadn't seemed keen about.

Nevertheless, because the mission house in Temuco was occupied at the time, it wasn't until early the following year that eventually they were able to move in. In spite of this, Doug could now begin taking Spanish services in Temuco.

Meanwhile, Tony, thinking back to his veterinary days in Ilfracombe and the successful youth club he had run there with Doug, had started one in Chol Chol. This also flourished, so he agreed to send over a strong delegation to help Doug launch a similar club in Temuco. This was to be held each Sunday afternoon. It also proved very successful as more and more Mapuche youths began to come in from the surrounding countryside. They would then stay on to attend the evening service. By the time the Milmines had moved into Temuco, this had built up to about eighty members. So at last we were seeing some of our plans for the Mapuches coming to pass.

We now decided to widen our horizons to include ministry among Chileans as well as Mapuches. In order to clarify this new emphasis, we changed our name from 'The Araucanian Mission' to 'The Anglican Mission'. So gradually, over our ten years in Chile, we were able to open centres in several other of the major cities such as Concepción, Santiago, Valparaiso and Viña del Mar. Here we soon attracted educated Chileans to help us in our task. After several years in Temuco, the Milmines themselves graciously agreed to leave their beloved home there to start up a new Spanish speaking centre in the capital, Santiago.

In sickness and in health

A MONTH after our arrival in Chol Chol, our commitment had been seriously put to the test. I had noticed an angry flea bite on the top of little Hilary's foot. After taking the usual precautions I hoped it would clear up but it rapidly turned nasty and her leg began to swell. So I took her along to the hospital where they gave me M & B tablets. But gradually it got worse, the swelling increased and the skin became tense and dreadfully discoloured. Her temperature soared, so clearly the tablets weren't enough.

When Miss Royce came to visit her the next morning, she was appalled at what she found. With her voice choking with emotion she explained that, with her limited resources, there was just nothing more she could do; she feared that Hilary might die before we could get further help. For the first time I felt total despair. With baby on my lap, her breathing now scarcely perceptible, we wept and prayed together.

Meanwhile Tony, who was in Temuco and unaware of her worsening condition, felt strangely moved to buy some Penicillin. On riding back, he was dismayed to see how bad she had become and so immediately got Miss Royce to inject her with it. This undoubtedly saved her life, as from then on she gradually recovered. Once again, the Lord had heard and answered our prayers, but in a most unexpected way.

Just after this we all went down with severe hepatitis; all except Hilary, that is. If she had caught it I don't think she would have survived, as she was still very frail from her blood poisoning.

Terry was the first to succumb. He felt so rotten that I kept him in bed. Four days later we knew why! He went a sickly yellow – it was jaundice, or hepatitis. Rosemary followed two weeks later, but much milder. It was only when the next day Tony and I also went down with it that life became really difficult. We were both extremely ill.

I was bad, but fortunately not quite as bad as Tony. Hearing Hilary crying from her room I was just about able to crawl along the corridor to comfort her. I found her lying on a soggy mattress in her cot with a big patch of white on the floor where the acid from her urine had burnt off the polish. This kick started me into action and I forced myself to keep going, come what may. For three whole weeks Tony could not even keep down water, yet alone food. He just kept on vomiting with nothing to bring up. By then he looked like a walking skeleton.

Dear Miss Royce did the best she could. She insisted, 'Tony, whatever you do you must not worry!' But with the next breath, 'Tony, my man can't shoe my horse because there are no horse shoes.' Then, 'Why haven't you written to London yet to insist that they send out the funds'. It seemed that every time she appeared she had some new problem for Tony to solve, but it was always followed by the refrain, 'Tony, you just must not worry'.

Her pet remedy for anything to do with the liver was Boldo, a local herb much prized in such cases. This was cheap, easy to administer and perfectly disgusting to drink. Far from stopping the vomiting, we heaved at the slightest thought of the next dose. So Tony went on strike; but all to no avail. His nurse was far too sharp. She soon noticed that the bottle was not going down and severely reprimanded him. In future she would watch the levels to make sure that he began to take it. 'You'll never get better, if you don't take your Boldo' she insisted. So, no sooner had she left the house than Tony rallied sufficiently to stagger to the bathroom and pour the next dose down the loo. From then on he slowly improved!

I felt that somehow I had to get him away from this situation

so that he really couldn't worry. As I described earlier, help came when our friends in Concepción; Peter and Elsie Tadman, invited us to spend a time of convalescence with them.

Some time later, we had another scare. Once my tummy had gone down after Pattie's birth, I noticed a huge lump in my abdomen. Tony palpated it and was very alarmed. The first thing that crossed our minds was the possibility of a cancerous growth. The doctor we consulted also thought the same but advised us to get a second opinion. So we went to a doctor of German descent who was sure that it was my gall bladder. Accordingly he operated in Temuco hospital. I came round to find a box of 90 stones of all shapes and sizes. The doctor told me that the gall bladder would probably have split under the weight had I not had the operation. I knew he was telling the truth because he had let one of our mission nurses assist him. To go the second mile, he had also taken out my appendix to avoid any further crisis, as we lived so far out in the country. For all this he would charge us no fee; only asking for the equivalent of £5.00 for his anaesthetist.

Knowing we were trying to help the poor Mapuches and that I would have had a long journey to bring them into the hospital, he would allow me to jump the queue and take them straight into Casualty. One such case was a Mapuche lady called Señora Aurora who used to visit me. She was fascinated by our Pattie and said how she so longed to have a baby of her own. After quite a while, she appeared one day and told me happily that she thought at last she was expecting a little one. She certainly looked as if she was. So I asked, 'When do you think its due?' She looked rather vague and replied, 'Well, its since the last harvest I think.' So as we were just coming to the next harvest I said, 'I think we had better go into Temuco to see my doctor'. The doctor kept her in and operated. Sadly, it turned out to be a big cyst and as far as I know she never did have her baby. Again the doctor wouldn't charge. Incidentally, his grandson is now a member of Terry's congregation in Viña del Mar.

Another nasty medical fright that we had was when Pattie, now two years old, had a heavy cold that suddenly turned to acute pneumonia. The only room we could warm, apart from the kitchen, was our little living/dining room. So we brought down two mattresses and kept her there with us day and night in the warmth of the log fire. Her rasping breathing got so bad that we could hear it from the kitchen. Imagine our joy and amazement when just as suddenly as it had started, her breathing became normal again. The crisis had passed and she was soon fit and well.

Actually, all five of our children, except Terry, had life threatening illnesses or accidents while we were in Chile. Even Terry took a great lump of flesh out of his leg when in basketball he jumped against the post that had a nasty bolt sticking out of it. But this was not life threatening. After we moved on to Quepe we nearly lost both Rosemary and Jonnie (our youngest).

Tony also had several brushes with a number of deadly diseases. For example during one particularly dreadful nation-wide outbreak of rabies he was walking down the street when a little dog shot out from a house and bit him in the heel, drawing blood. This was obviously a very serious matter, so he immediately went to the local hospital for an injection, only to be told that they were completely out of serum due to the heavy run on it. Even in the capital, Santiago, there wasn't any. It was a long and anxious few weeks, waiting for the incubation period to run its course, before we knew that he had been spared.

Years later, in the Argentine, Jonnie (our youngest) had a friend at the nearby kiosk. Their pet bulldog was ill and so he asked his dad if he would look at it, as they were too poor to pay the fees of the local vet. Tony felt that it was a typical case of rabies but in handling it some of the saliva got on his hand where he had a small open cut. There was only one thing for it, a series of unpleasant injections. To save him going in and out of the clinic, I managed to persuade them to let me have the serum and I was able to inject these at home. This was just as well because the dog died and a post mortem test confirmed that this time it was rabies.

Perhaps the most deadly outbreak of disease we encountered was among the rural Mapuches; it was typhus. As soon as he heard, Tony visited the affected areas. What he saw was too dreadful for words. In each community a large proportion of the population had been struck down. In every ruca that he visited, there were sick and dying, stretched out inert on the ground. Some were even dead, awaiting burial. Some of our close friends perished. Throughout, the fortitude of the new Christians was remarkable. It was one thing to make a public profession of faith in Christ, but quite another to stand firm while being battered by the winds of affliction.

At the General Conference, Don Samuel Maripán, a very new Christian, told his story of how only two months before he had been brought back from the very jaws of death. Here is a literal translation of what he said.

'My dear brothers and sisters in Christ, the Pastor has asked me to speak about my time of sickness. It was in August that I fell sick. I was very ill and nearly died of typhus, that terrible sickness which suddenly arrived in our area. I was willing to die and had much faith in Christ; my heart altogether depended on Him. The Pastor came to visit me one day and this gave me more faith. I don't remember very much of what happened to me in those days, but I know that I was always praying. I also asked my brothers in Christ to pray for me. After fifteen days I was able to remember a few things and at the end of twenty days I was better and got up. Because of this, my dear brothers, I must say that if any one has his faith in Christ it is a great blessing; I didn't fear to die but only asked, 'When will the Lord take me to glory?' I know that I nearly died, but by the grace of God I'm with you in this Conference today.'

At first, the Mapuches were so suspicious of the Chilean Health Authorities that they refused to co-operate with their control measures. Frustrated, the officials appealed to Tony. They knew that the Mapuches trusted our mission and asked him if he would intervene by trying to persuade them that they were reliable. Fortunately, they listened and believed him and so the outbreak was brought under control much more quickly than would otherwise have been possible.

We always felt that the sad experience of our children's illnesses had prepared us to share more sympathetically in the sorrows of others, especially when little children were concerned. For example, when visiting one very poor family, I discovered that the mother, Señora Parra, was a widow with several children to feed. One of these was a tiny child, wrapped up in old clothes. I was told her name was Rosita. But the baby's haunting, weak cry quite worried me. The Señora told me that she was looking after Rosita because her mother had died of T.B. On the table was a baby's bottle containing ground wheat in water. The teat of the bottle was covered with flies.

While we were talking, she began to unwrap the bundle of rags and I was horrified at Rosita's little body. I had never seen anything quite so distressing, not even in pictures of the concentration camps. Her stomach was dreadfully distended; her legs and arms mere sticks, literally just bones covered with loose skin. I was so disturbed that I offered to take her home and look after her for a while.

I immediately started feeding her with very diluted Nestlé's Milk and then gradually went on to Nido. When I was bathing her, I saw that her head was full of ulcers, so I dressed it with ointment from the hospital; I then made, and put on, little bonnets that I burnt each day. Gradually her head cleared up. She was also very chesty and as her mother had died of TB I feared the worst. So I kept her in a separate room to avoid infecting our children.

She had the most beautiful, brown eyes which soon began to follow me around the room. As she got stronger, she lifted up her little head as well. She was putting on weight and improving fast when we had to go away for a few weeks. Regretfully I handed her back to Sra Parra, giving her tins of Nido to continue feeding her.

As soon as I got back I hurried round to see how she was. I was told that she had returned to her mother's family and was all right. However, a month later I was passing when I spotted Rosita on a little table. She was laid out, dead. She looked so peaceful but just like a little old lady, weary with life.

We had her funeral in our church and the following day we took her to the cemetery, sad but relieved that at last she was at peace. It transpired that the milk I left for her had been used for the other children, but who could blame these poor, impoverished people.

A few months after little Rosita's funeral, Julia, the lady who cooked so well for the Señoritas over in the Girls' Boarding School, was off on maternity leave. She started giving birth one afternoon in the middle of winter but soon after began haemorrhaging. She was taken over to the hospital where Miss Royce diagnosed the serious condition of placenta previa.

That night she was a little better, but the next morning, in spite of all the midwife could do, she was still bleeding badly. The following afternoon she was no better. The weather was appalling; the rain had been bucketing down for days and all the rivers were in spate. Miss Royce was in a dilemma. The difficulty of getting Julia to Temuco was almost insuperable and yet to leave her another day seemed even worst. So at 4 p.m. she made the vital decision, Julia would have to be taken to the hospital in Temuco. Her husband Florencio and her brother Augustin were the obvious choices to accompany Tony and Nurse Maud on this hazardous journey.

Julia was put on a stretcher and gently lifted into a covered ox-cart. Maud was seated at her side in constant attendance. Augustin drove the ox-cart while Tony, wading on foot waist deep in the seething floodwater, carried the Tilly Lamp. This lamp was fuelled by compressed paraffin that heated a delicate mantle to white heat. The light was quite bright and was essential, as by now it was pitch dark. Florencio, also on foot,

probed the ground with a long pole to alert the cart driver of any large holes underneath the surface. They were heading for the river Imperial where they hoped the ambulance that Maud had phoned would be awaiting them on the other side.

Their first major hazard was a small wooden bridge just outside the village. All that could be seen of it was the top of the two flimsy balustrades peeping above the fierce flow of the river. Whether the planks of the bridge itself were still there or not was impossible to tell. Poor Augustin took one look at it and decided to turn back. This, of course, meant that Florencio now had to drive the cart, giving no pre-warning of major gullies ahead. They each said a little prayer in their hearts as they ploughed on.

Florencio aimed at a point mid-way between the two balustrades and gingerly edged across. The rest of the journey was an absolute nightmare. Time and time again Tony was half swept off his feet by the terrific force of the water. The worst moment was when he and the light actually part fell under the water. The light fizzed and then went out leaving them all in total darkness. Afterwards, the ambulance men told them that when they saw the light disappear they were about to leave as they thought they must have turned back. But suddenly, and quite miraculously, the lamp gave a splutter and the light re-ignited and they were saved. At 8.30 p.m. they at last reached the river Imperial. They were relieved to see the lights of the ambulance waiting for them over the river on the hard gravel road.

A tiny boat was launched from the other side. When it arrived, Julia's stretcher exactly fitted, within inches. They all travelled in the ambulance until Imperial where Tony and Maud stayed the night in a boarding house. The ambulance then took Julia and Florencio straight on to the hospital in Temuco where they arrived at about 11 p.m. and she was safely delivered of a baby girl.

After supper Tony and Maud went to their respective rooms. Tony, having handed out his soaking clothes to the staff to dry for the morning, fell into bed totally exhausted. In the morning, eager for his breakfast, he couldn't leave his room without clothes and so yelled for help. Whether as a practical joke or by design, no one came to his rescue. At last, after a superhuman bellow, Maud heard and, overcome with embarrassment, timidly placed his dried clothes into a desperate hand that came groping around the door.

The next day the worst of the flooding had subsided, so after phoning Chol Chol for horses, they hired a car to take them back to the river for 250 pesos. Having crossed in the same small boat, they found the man with the horses waiting and so they all rode safely back to Chol Chol.

When they came to the submerged bridge, where Augustin had turned back, they discovered that he had had good reason! The planks on one side had been completely washed away. They had passed safely on the narrow strip that was still intact. Otherwise, of course, ox-cart and all would have been swept away in the torrent.

What with our illnesses and those of others, we certainly have had our fair share of the sorrows of sickness. In our marriage vows, we had pledged our love in sickness and in health. God's faithfulness had allowed us to keep true to our promises, both then and indeed right up to the day I write.

CHAPTER THIRTEEN

Vice, violence and victory

AS WE'VE seen, our family enjoyed taking part in the Chilean fiestas; however, there was a down side. The fiestas were times when many drank to excess, often to the extent of being so far gone that they were rolling about in the gutter. Miss Royce was particularly severe in her condemnation of what she considered to be a mindless vice which caused many unnecessary accidents and deaths. Every year we heard of a number of drunken horsemen that had been swept away and drowned when attempting to cross a river, so I think she was right. If a drunk had the misfortune to pass her in the street she would shake her finger accusingly at him and in her sternest voice urge him to turn from his evil ways. As she had treated most of them in their childhood, she obviously felt that she had a vested interest in their well-being. The poor unfortunate culprit would freeze with fright, like a rabbit caught in the headlights of a car.

After all, she was the one who had to patch them up! On fiesta days, the outpatients department at her hospital would have a long queue of shamefaced victims of knife fights. They knew what to expect from Miss Royce! With this type of case she could be pretty ruthless, stitching them up without a local anaesthetic and with only the blunt reminder, 'You have had your anaesthetic already, so you certainly don't need another!' One could hear their yells from quite a distance. Then she would demand that they take off their poncho and hand it over. She would only return it if they came back the next day sober, when she would give them a stiff ticking off.

One of the victims of drink was our delightful little gardener called Chureo. There was a cultivated plot of land that went with our house that provided us with vegetables and an abundance of sweet and juicy strawberries. To look after the garden, we employed this funny little man as a part-time gardener. He looked just like a Chinaman, especially in his straw gardening hat. Hilary was so fond of him, and he of her. She spent lots of time with him, being pushed around in his wheelbarrow.

His one failing was that on fiesta days he too would drink to excess. If he turned up drunk for work this could cause serious problems with the school children. Tony pleaded with him to break with the habit, as otherwise he would have no option but to dismiss him because of his responsibility towards the school children. Alas, in spite of all our warnings on fiesta days he was still unable to resist. So, with a very heavy heart, we had at last to dismiss him. To our distress we learnt some time later that he had been found drowned in a water-trough after another bout of drinking. This was one of our most painful memories that saddened us for many days to come.

We did everything in our power to warn the people against the evils of drinking to excess. On fiesta days we would go down to the football ground and preach in the open air, as John Wesley had done when England had been in a similar condition. He had found that the message of the Gospel had the power to transform the lives of people who were slaves to drink, so why should it not do the same in Chile? After all, we were hearing of the same kind of miracles occurring daily in Billy Graham's giant rallies in England.

Sure enough, we too began to see the same kind of results; drunkards and others began yielding their lives to Christ and were being transformed by his power. Men who had previously been brutal wife-beaters were changing into loving, kind and responsible husbands and fathers.

One such was Don Segundo Morales. He worked in the local mill and so if you passed him in the street he was usually well dusted with flour. But he was one of the drunkards in Chol Chol. His addiction had gradually drained his home of all its furniture, but his poor wife and children could do nothing about it. The pull of his drinking 'friends' had him enslaved. He was helpless to break out.

Then he suddenly surrendered his shattered life to Christ. He began to attend the services in our church. This, in itself was an amazing act of courage. On the way, he had to pass several of his previous drinking haunts where his old 'friends' came out to jeer at him and urge him to come back to join them; but Segundo quietly passed by.

He now began to use his wages from the mill to buy good food, to replace the furniture, and the other essential household utensils. One of the first things he did was to go to the hospital to buy a large bottle of Cod Liver Oil for his children. He bought a Bible and began to teach the stories to his children. Surrounded by the loving support of his new Christian friends, he gradually climbed out of the terrible pit. The whole family was transformed. By the time we left Chol Chol, he was helping others to safety. So we were seeing that the Gospel had the power to change lives in Chile, as it had done in England in the days of Wesley.

At the same time we were experiencing similar cases in the rural areas. One outstanding example of this occurred in a place called Pitraco. It all started as a result of the terrible typhus outbreak that I described in the last chapter. We had been making occasional visits to this place where a small group of people used to gather in the open-air to listen. The little children especially liked the stories about Jesus. One Sunday, a Mapuche called Ramón Coñuepán came into town requesting a funeral service in our church for his four-year-old child who had died of typhus. Apparently, when he was in the agonies of death he had asked that he might be taken to the church in Chol Chol for the funeral, as it was there that eternal healing could be found in Jesus. The next morning Tony took the funeral. Here we had good opportunities to speak to the people who were so interested. Ramón told us that this was his second child to die recently of typhus. It was very touching to be told that this little fellow had actually died on his fourth birthday.

Three weeks later, Ramón came down again. He gave Tony a warm abrazo (Chilean hug of greeting) and said he and his wife now wished to follow Christ; also that all his neighbours in Pitraco were interested to have this message explained to them more fully. It was a great joy to help them to make their decision to leave their old life and start a new one following the Lord Jesus Christ.

From this small beginning, things just grew and grew. A month later, Tony rode up to Pitraco for a teaching session with the Coñuepán family. Not only his own family wanted to follow in the same way, but now there was a group of Chileans who did also. One of these was the family of Rómulo Cartes. This was quite amazing as this mixed community was noted for the most bitter racial hatred between Mapuches and Chileans; this would constantly flare up and boil over into violence.

As the group grew, they decided to build a modest little place where they could worship together. Ramón invited Tony up to inaugurate his new 'church'. It was a nice structure, built of straw as a ruca is. He had visited all his friends and invited them to attend so there was a good crowd waiting.

We were especially pleased when Ramón came to tell us that he and the woman he lived with wanted to get married and asked Tony if he would take the service. To us these marriages were very important. They were gradually replacing very loose relationships with much more stable and loving ones. Of course, the children where the great beneficiaries. It was also a delight when Ramón told his story to the General Conference of how a little child had led them; from this child's faith a whole new church had been brought to birth.

However, as unity between the two races within the church continued to grow, so did the fierce resistance from without.

Ramón's own sister, who was a Machi (a Mapuche witchdoctor), said that the deaths of his two children from typhus were a punishment for his friendship with the hated Chileans. One Sunday afternoon at the end of May, two of our national leaders set off for Pitraco to visit the church there. As they approached they found Rómulo Cartes, the Chilean, lying in a pool of blood from an axe wound in his head. Ramón Coñuepán, the Mapuche, immediately put him in his ox-cart and brought him down to us. When Tony saw how bad he was, he raced him into our hospital for treatment. Each day he visited and prayed with him there. When he began to improve, Rómulo poured out the whole sordid story of how one of the hostile Mapuches had cornered him, a Chilean, and in his hatred had attacked him with an axe, leaving him for dead.

The carabineros went straight up to Pitraco and arrested the Mapuche attacker, Juan Neculeo, who confessed to attempted murder. They brought him down to Chol Chol where they put him in a cell. The next week, Rómulo was a little better, so Tony suggested that together they might visit Juan in prison. They found him in a very sorry state: cold, hungry, and dejected. During his week in hospital Rómulo had decided that, as a Christian, he should forgive Juan. He now put this into practice by offering to get him food and drink. The effect was extraordinary; seeing such love in his former enemy completely broke Juan down. Weeping, he said he too wanted to accept Christ, so in front of the astonished carabineros Tony prayed with him as he did so.

The next day, Juan asked God to get him out of prison; the following morning one of the carabineros came in and said, 'You can go, Juan!'. He could scarcely believe his ears and set off for home rejoicing. On the way, he bumped into Rómulo who immediately urged him to return to Chol Chol to tell the Pastor what had happened to him. As Tony was out, I received them and took them along to one of our leaders. After recounting the whole wonderful story, the two former enemies set off once more for Pitraco rejoicing together at what God had done in both their lives.

But did these transformations last? We had proof enough of their reality and abiding nature when forty-five years later Terry, our son, revisited Chol Chol. There he met Ramón Coñuepán and Rómulo Cartes and they were still close friends and rejoicing in Christ. We have a lovely photograph of the three of them just to remind us of the wonderful fact that, if we'll let him, the Lord can heal racial hatred too!

Then there was the case of Panguilef Loncovil. Perhaps his was not the most spectacular of these changes but undoubtedly it was one of the deepest and most influential. Tony first met him when he was riding back from one of the rural churches. He had caught up with a horseman wending his way home and got into conversation with him. They were soon discussing the importance of having a strong faith in the Lord Jesus Christ. Obviously God had prepared the heart of this young teenager as he responded with joy to the good news of Christ. Like so many of the Mapuches, Panguilef had severe pulmonary T.B. and was admitted into the Chol Chol hospital where he found health for his body and strength for his new faith.

When we left for our first home leave, Tony especially asked Bill Flagg, who was to replace us in Chol Chol, if he would do all he could to help Pangui who had an insatiable appetite for further learning. Bill was able to arrange for special tuition in secondary education and this certainly paid off. Later Bill reported, and I quote, 'Twenty years later, he (Panguilef), as a university professor, would give me the place of honour at a meal to celebrate the graduation of his eldest son from primary school. The boy went on to obtain the first place in the national university entrance examinations in chemistry. Pangui, who was not ordained, became a wonderful man of encouragement and counsel across the future diocese. He served for 25 years as general secretary of the Diocesan Executive Council and played a crucial role in the development of the diocesan education work, including a school for deaf people in Temuco, before he died in his forties.'

After we had retired, on one of our several three-monthly return trips to Chile to help our SEAN team in Viña, we met up again with dear Panguilef. As Bill reported, he was by now a man of some educational stature, an amazing achievement for a Mapuche lad from such an impoverished background. But we found him the same humble, unassuming Christian that we had always known. His brilliant career had not spoilt him one bit. Shortly after this he went to be with his Lord.

CHAPTER FOURTEEN

From rivalry to reconciliation

DURING OUR time in Chol Chol, relationships between our Mission and that of the Roman Catholics were sadly strained. The local priest, a North American, called Padre Jaime seemed to feel threatened by the rapid growth of our churches. Also he appeared to resent the fact that our mission had been founded in 1895 and was extremely well established by the time they arrived in Chol Chol years later. This resentment developed into an unsavoury rivalry that we bitterly regretted.

Things weren't helped by the fact that in those days Roman Catholicism in South America combined genuine Christian faith with pagan practices. On one such occasion groups of Catholics would go round the houses asking for donations towards a party called 'the cross of May'. The penalty for refusal to co-operate was a solemn curse on your house and garden. Tony refused to co-operate on the grounds that our resources were limited and that any spare cash went on alleviating the needs of others.

Now it so happened that we had brought out a packet of broad-bean seed from England being unaware at the time that this was strictly prohibited in Chile. In all innocence, we had planted them in our garden and they were beginning to sprout.

These beans seemed oblivious to the curse and just kept on growing in spite of it. As news leaked out about their remarkable size, our beans became the talk of the town. Villagers would shyly turn up on our doorstep pleading for a few to plant as seed in their own gardens. After a year or two, half the village was harvesting abundant crops of this much sort-after variety. Tony was just a bit naughty; he said he was tempted to offer a small donation to their funds if they would agree to come back and curse our garden again.

This opposition to our work steadily intensified. Now the processions began cursing one-by-one our rural churches as well. I'm glad to say this was equally ineffective as they went on growing too. With this regrettable rivalry, it was all the more surprising when one day Tony bumped into Padre Jaime outside a village shop. He drew Tony furtively to one side and said earnestly, 'I've been wanting to speak to you for some time. What is the secret behind so many people being turned from vice and violence to become good, sober citizens? How can this be explained?' This led to an extraordinary chain of events continuing to the present day.

Breaking with all previous protocol in Chol Chol, Tony offered to visit Jaime in his large mission compound on the other side of the village. In the prevailing climate, if this meeting had got out it could have been extremely damaging to both their reputations. However, Tony and I felt that it was the right thing to do and so in the dead of night he crept into Jaime's domain! There they had a prolonged discussion on the similarity of what was going on in Chol Chol to that of the lives of those transformed in the early days of the church as reported in the Acts of the Apostles. As Tony knew that Jaime had been trained in the USA he had assumed that he would be well-versed in the New Testament accounts of these events; to his astonishment he discovered that he was completely ignorant of them.

This led to a series of clandestine meetings between the two. By arrangement, Jaime would walk far along the riverbank to a secluded spot; a quarter of an hour later, Tony would nonchalantly saunter along to the same spot hoping that no one would spot him.

This friendship developed into a prolonged correspondence on the matter. Poor Jaime was confused; on the one hand he realised that the New Testament history of the early church must still be relevant, on the other he could not understand how this could be happening in a church that he had been taught was apostate. At last in desperation he burst out, 'Well! Even though I don't have an answer to these things myself I will certainly get an answer from those that do'. The following day he disappeared. He must have gone to his higher authority, who decided to remove him from Chol Chol. He returned a year later as hard as nails and unwilling to engage in any further conversation.

There things rested for the remainder of our time in South America. It was only after we had retired to our family cottage in Seaton, that we got news of him again. Apparently, Jaime had left the priesthood in order to return to Chol Chol and dedicate the rest of his life to helping the impoverished Mapuches. To raise support for this work, he had set up a project named the 'Chol Chol Foundation'. Sadly, after years of sacrificial service, he had eventually died of advanced emphysema. We then recalled how during our time in Chol Chol, he had been a chain smoker. Indeed, Tony had often urged him to kick the deadly habit. Sadly he had been unable to do so and now it had claimed his life.

Just before hearing this sad news, Terry had to visit again his old haunts in Chol Chol. The first thing he did was to seek out Jaime, to see how he was. We were so sorry to learn that he arrived too late. Jaime had just died and his funeral had taken place the day before Terry arrived. It was lovely to learn, however, that the Mapuches had come from near and far to pack the church at his funeral, so greatly was he missed and loved.

Then, quite out of the blue, we got a call from two of Jaime's friends from the south of Chile who were over in England. They wanted to write a book about his life in his memory and wondered if we could provide further details of those early days in Chol Chol. They then revealed the astonishing information that they had found all the letters Tony had sent Jaime those many years ago carefully filed away among his effects. Apparently he had treasured them greatly.

But the best was yet to come. At the time of writing this

book, Hilary's children (the Cooper family) have been taking part in a special project to help build new houses for the Mapuches, near Chol Chol. This scheme was called the 'Chol Chol Foundation'. It was none other than the project Jaime had started.

On the latest of these journeys Jahnn and his younger sister Melanie took part. Melanie has just visited Tony and me in England, immediately after returning from her trip and so was able to give us first hand news, illustrated by the photos she had taken, of all their adventures.

She reported how their group had been about seventy strong. They were divided into seven 'communities' or teams and each team was to build three homes. These would be small, wooden pre-fab houses, a great improvement on their existing outdated straw huts (rucas). Although warm, a ruca is extremely uncomfortable and most unhealthy. It consists of a single room in which all the family activities are carried out. It is usually full of fleas, animals and, above all, smoke. This latter is due to the open fire always burning in the middle of the floor, in summer as well as winter, as all the household cooking is done on this. There are no windows nor a chimney, the smoke escaping from a single hole in the apex of the tapered roof. Consequently, the walls are blackened by years of soot and cobwebs.

On arrival, after the long train journey south, they were taken directly to their main base, a large boarding school with two dormitories, one for the girls and the other for the boys. After lunch each team was driven to their respective area and introduced to the families that were to receive the new houses. Jahnn was one of the team drivers and so after lunch he drove Melanie and her team the forty-five-minute journey to their three families.

It was certainly hard and dirty work. Before anything could be built, the ground had to be levelled. As there was no shade and the heat was intense, the dust blew up into their faces. Furthermore, on the back of the van they had already been covered in dust on the journey. By the end of the day they were filthy. Then they were told that regretfully the water-tank was so low that they would have to be strictly rationed to one shower per fortnight! Not the kind of thing the young Señoritas were used to! Melanie herself is a good example of getting her priorities right on these matters. She is one of the models for a well-known designer firm in Santiago; her life size photos are seen in most of the big fashion shops there. All the more credit to her and her friends that they not only pitched into the mud and grime with good will, but also enjoyed it.

At base, the teams took it in turns to do the various chores, washing up, cooking the breakfast, and, perhaps the most difficult, rousing their sleeping companions for the day's duties. For this last, they had an ingenious scheme. Each team was to think up the most novel method to ensure that everyone got up on time. As you can imagine, some of these turned out to be quite unpleasant, even if effective. So when it came to Melanie's team, they felt that everyone had had their fill of nasty methods and so decided on something really nice. Rising early, they went out into the fields to pick a few of the most beautiful flowers that they could find. Then each sleeper was gently nudged awake and immediately presented with a lovely bloom, all to the sound of gentle music! Miraculously it worked! Also at the end of the week, their team had gained the maximum number of brownie points and were acclaimed as the best.

Once the houses were completed, they all united in a farewell ceremony. Each team was seated with their three new homeowners. A special crèche was organised to look after the Mapuche children, letting their parents enjoy to the full the meal and ceremony. Each family was presented with a beautiful diploma as they were passed the keys of their new home. It was a time of deep emotion as the young group said farewell to the people they had helped so nicely and to whom they had become so attached.

When we, as grandparents, heard this account we were

overjoyed to see how our grandchildren were carrying on the work that had been so dear to both Jaime and to us. Apparently, they have now been organising these aid expeditions for five years and have built approximately eighty houses.

So, by a wonderful act of providence, the wheel has turned full circle. With the kids' participation in Jaime's project, both Tony and I feel that our reconciliation with our old adversary is now complete.

CHAPTER FIFTEEN

Perils galore ...

WE HAD four main forms of travel to get in and out of Chol Chol: ox-cart, tractor and trailer, lorry and finally, and most efficiently, horseback. Later, Doug was able to buy the Land Rover from Peter Tadman and we were donated a Unimog (tractor cum jeep) which greatly facilitated our travel in all weathers. When we got to Paraguay, practically the only way we could visit the Enthlit community in the Chaco was in a tiny Cessna aeroplane. There, most of the indigenous people had never seen a car!

In Chol Chol, the most primitive and slowest of our means of transport was the ox-cart. Yet it could take much heavier loads than a horse and, unlike lorries or cars, could get through the thickest mud. You may remember that it was in an ox-cart that Julia, the cook, passed safely through the floodwaters on her way to Temuco to get medical help with the birth of her baby.

The tractor and trailer was a little faster than an ox-cart, but slightly more dangerous. On one such occasion Tony, Pattie and I had to travel on this trailer along with a bench and circular saw, needed to cut our year's supply of logs in Chol Chol. The heavy bench was placed down the centre of the trailer, leaving us hanging on around the sides. Over one of the very deep ruts, the whole contraption tipped sideways, shooting Tony, with Pattie in his arms, to the ground. For one dreadful moment I lay across the bench looking down on them. I scrambled off as quickly as possible so that the driver could attempt to straighten the vehicle. When I climbed on again, in no way could we persuade Pattie to follow. So Tony had to walk the rest of the journey, carrying her in his arms. Fortunately we were not too far from home when this accident occurred.

In the summer, when the roads were dry, we could pay to travel by lorry; this of course was much faster. However, it was not as comfortable as you might think. If, as usual, we were sitting on planks at the back, we were choked by dense clouds of dust. When I had to take baby Pattie with me, I would put her in a partially zipped up holdall, with her face under the open end, covered by a muslin nappy to keep out the dust. On arrival, I would breast feed and change her. Struggles would then take out a drawer where she would fit snugly on a pillow. Once she was asleep, I would slip out and do my shopping before returning for lunch and then catching the lorry back.

Even the lorry could prove unpredictable. On one such return journey, we broke down half way! We had run out of petrol. The Chileans jokingly refer to this as a 'panne de tonto' which means 'breakdown of an idiot!' So the 'idiot' driver trotted off happily with an empty petrol can, which he kept specially for these occasions, hoping to persuade some nearby farmer to sell him enough to get us home. As usual the back of the lorry was packed with a mixture of sacks, an assortment of animals (such as chickens or a sheep) and of course the ubiquitous drunken men. A group of these was flirting with a couple of girls. They had opened a large demijohn of strong drink and were offering this for sale. By now, I felt things were getting out of hand and so I offered to buy the lot. I intended to tip it out in an attempt to defuse the situation. They must have read my thoughts as my offer was turned down! Mercifully, at that moment the driver returned with enough petrol to get us back to Chol Chol.

The fourth and most versatile form of travel was on horseback. This was the way Tony did nearly all his rural visiting. On our arrival, he had been allocated a beautiful black mare. She could walk, trot, canter and gallop, but he now taught her how to pace. With this gait, on the flat, she could keep going mile after mile at a speed similar to a canter; and this, even in the mud. She was noted for getting him into Temuco in all weathers, in record time. Horsemen nearly always rode in pairs or groups in those days; it was considered far too dangerous to ride alone. But such was the respect in which our founders had been held that we could move about without fear. So Tony usually rode alone and was never attacked.

When preparing to go to veterinary college, he had enrolled in a nearby riding school. A fierce looking cavalry officer with waxed military moustache ran this. His theory was that each student had to fall off; better to do so in his soft sawdust ring than on the hard road outside. He waited for an unguarded moment and then flicked the rump of Tony's horse with his great whip. Of course, the horse reared up, lurched violently to one side, and sent him flying.

However, this training, tough as it was, must have worked. In all the thousands of miles he rode in Chile, over every kind of difficult terrain, he only fell twice. On both occasions this was because the horse itself fell under him. None of his lady colleagues had had the benefit of going to riding school; their training was in the harder school of experience. Sadly they all were thrown on different occasions.

I suppose Muriel Parrott sustained the worst of these falls. She had been visiting in Temuco and had informed us that she would be returning to Chol Chol that afternoon. As it got darker and she had not arrived we began to get worried. On phoning Temuco we were told that she had left at 2.30 p.m. so we decided to send out a search-party; Don Germán and Tony set off in the dark to look for her. The further they went the more concerned they became; there was no sign of her and no one they asked had seen her either. After riding well over half way to Temuco, they started asking for news in the houses along the roadside. At last a lad told them that she had taken the wrong fork; this was the reason why no one had seen her on our road. Apparently, the horse she had been riding had bolted; it had veered off the track and hit a wire fence at full speed. Muriel had been catapulted forward and hit the ground 10 yards away.

Some kind neighbours who saw this happen had picked her up and taken her into hospital in Temuco in an ox-cart. They had also taken care of her horse. As there was nothing more that they could do, Tony and Don Germán collected her horse and rode back to Chol Chol, arriving at 2.30 a.m. next morning. Eventually we received news by telephone that Muriel was in bed with serious concussion and would be there for at least two weeks.

Of course, Tony wasn't immune to accidents when out riding. He very nearly came to grief when his heavily loaded saddlebags, which had not been tightened sufficiently, slipped and twisted under the mare's belly, flapping back and forth as she bolted. The faster she galloped the more terrified she became. She left the road, jumping deep gullies and low hedges. Tony frantically tried to get her under control while at the same time reaching down in an effort to heave the saddle bags back into position. At last he succeeded in pulling her up and was able to dismount to readjust the slackened girths.

On another occasion when he was visiting Juan Neculeo, Ramón Coñuepán and Rómulo Cartes in Pitraco, he was crossing country on a route he didn't know. The track suddenly took a surprise loop around what appeared to be a swath of grass. Being late for his appointment, he decided to leave the road and cut across this 'grass'. His mare refused and shied away but he forced her to cross. Before going more than a few strides, he quickly discovered his mistake. The mare plunged up to her belly in quicksand.

He managed to climb on to the saddle and thrust towards the shore, landing half in and half out of the bog. Slowly he was able to crawl back on to firm land, still clutching the reins. By this time the mare was lying on her side, her head sinking fast. With the reins, he gently tugged, keeping her nostrils above the surface. The mare was thrashing about with her forelegs, trying to

107

find a firm footing. Suddenly she made contact with some roots at the side of the bog and eventually succeeded in scrambling back to safely. There they stood, man and beast side by side, trembling all over with exertion and relief. It was a very subdued Tony, covered in mud, that finally arrived that afternoon in Pitraco.

And so the perils went on. Several times Tony nearly got swept away in the torrent when fording rivers in spate. On another occasion, high up in the hills, he had to cross a swollen river in a dugout canoe, swimming his horse behind. I had to commit him to God's protection every time he went out alone.

As he was away so much, Tony felt he should keep one day a week free, so that he could spend quality time with me and the children. This proved to be more difficult than we had imagined. On his day off, I would be called to the front door by one of our rural teachers who had probably come in from miles away especially to see him. With beaming face he would ask for 'El Pastor', happily confident of a positive answer. He told me that he knew my husband would be there because someone had told him that this was his day off! My biggest problem was my conscience, which just wouldn't allow me to turn them away. So we decided it was better to keep on going and have peace of mind, than suffer the guilt of trying to deny what was obviously undeniable!

On a slightly lighter note was the four-hour horse-ride Tony made to Quepe at the request of Bill Flagg who had invited him to address a special meeting there. To reduce his riding time, he decided to go direct, cutting across country, rather than round the long way via Temuco. As he had never taken this route before, he was delayed several times, asking the way. At last he arrived and slipped in the back of the meeting, just as it was starting. He gave a little wave to Bill, who acknowledged with a smile.

An American, who had turned up by chance, was giving a 'short' report on his work. Tony was relieved, as this gave him a few moments to get his breath back after the tiring journey. However, he was not prepared for what happened. The visiting speaker went on…. and on….. and on…..! At last, when he concluded, Bill rose to his feet and thanked him effusively. Then to Tony's utter astonishment he calmly closed the meeting. In his euphoria, he had forgotten that Tony was to speak. When they greeted each other afterwards, first startled awareness, then dismay, hit Bill as he realised the enormity of his gaff. 'Horrors!' he gasped. 'Tony, I'm SO sorry.' Next morning, a rather disconsolate horseman plodded his weary way back to Chol Chol. When I asked him how he had got on, his wry grimace was a sufficient answer.

CHAPTER SIXTEEN

... But mission accomplished

ONE OF the reasons why Tony usually rode alone when visiting in the country was to allow his colleagues to visit some other places and thus multiply our effectiveness. But for this they would need training, so as soon as he could make himself understood in Spanish, Tony began to gather together a group of potential national leaders in a regular weekly leadership-training course. He and Muriel Parrot then devoted one evening a week to this. For Tony, this was the key to all that was to come. Early on, he had realised that with so many outlying centres, he could never reach them adequately without such an ever-growing team of nationals. These could share the load of helping new members and gaining others. He would therefore let nothing stand in his way. Riding back from a hard day in Temuco, he would leap from the saddle and rush over to take his evening lectures.

Soon this weekly leadership-training course began to pay off, as things gradually became more encouraging. As the group of leaders joined in the regular visitation of the rural centres these started to show fresh signs of life. Attendance, and then membership, began to grow. As a result, Tony was able to organise a series of week-long meetings.

These were mini-campaigns similar to those being conducted by Dr. Billy Graham, but on a far smaller scale. We decided to take three neighbouring schools at a time, starting with the most promising. The people from the other two were then invited to come along as well. This not only increased the attendance, but also the enthusiasm in the meetings.

In winter, these had to be held at night, after the people had finished their daylight duties. To offset the difficulty of travelling in the dark, we chose the period of full moon. On the next full moon, we moved to the second school, encouraging those who had responded in the first to throw in their weight behind us in the second. By the time we came to the third school, the momentum was considerable.

In those days the lamps used in the rucas were made from old Nestle Milk tins filled with paraffin and with a lighted rag-wick sticking out of it. Everyone who came to the meeting was asked to bring one of these. So as the family groups set out, we could see streams of twinkling lights, like fire-flies dancing in the night, as they eagerly converged on the central meeting place. Once assembled, it was surprising how these tiny lamps, when united, illuminated the whole room quite brightly.

In this way, we patiently covered all our schools, near and far. With a number of people having responded favourably to the message, the next step was the follow-up. Our trained leaders were now in their element. They could fan out in their visitation, greatly multiplying our potential. Chol Chol was becoming a really strong centre for a growing number of rural churches. The only thing that limited them was the number of horses available. As these were being over-used it was brought to Tony's attention that some of them had become seriously saddle sore. For a while everything had to slow down while he, putting on his veterinary hat again, had to treat them.

To encourage the new churches we now introduced an Annual General Conference in Chol Chol to which all from town and countryside were invited. This became one of the great events of the year especially for all our country folk who looked forward to it keenly. To give you some idea of what went on I'll describe the conference we held at the end of our third year in Chol Chol. Due to the phenomenal growth of the work, this year we expected a greater number than ever. We were not disappointed; seventy took advantage of the accommodation arranged for the three days and many others from the countryside came in daily to take part in the meetings.

I invite you, then, to let your imagination travel with me until you are attending the conference with us.

The first session is to begin at 2 p.m., but from 9 a.m. onwards the conferencistas from the surrounding rural areas begin to trickle in. The majority have come on foot, tired from their long journey. Some of these are very ragged and undernourished; others have come by horse and have a more prosperous appearance. All are keen to learn as much as possible and to enjoy catching up with all the news of their many friends. We join in the motley throng, perhaps feeling a little out of place in our European dress among all these ponchos and sombreros!

First we all pour into the conference office where we pay our quota towards our keep and expenses. The conference secretary marks off each name in her book. Some of us pay in cash, Chilean pesos, others in kind, such as eggs, beans, lentils etc. All of us emerge with a programme in our hand that gives details of the sessions and are labelled with a card that bears our name and locality. A friendly steward is waiting outside the door to conduct us to our respective dormitories.

The women are fortunate and find that they each have a wooden bedstead – no springs, but complete with mattress – in the girls' boarding school. The men are equally satisfied as they throw down their 'mantas' to reserve sleeping space on the huge communal straw 'bed' which covers the floor of the boys' dormitory. By the way, the 'manta' is a blanket usually hand-woven with a central slit through which the head is passed. It serves as an over-coat by day and as bedclothes by night.

After lunch we all troop into the conference room, jostling and laughing as we go; this is the large school hall packed with seats. The first thing that meets our eye is the portrait of the grand old pioneer, Daddy Wilson, founder of the work in Chol Chol. The theme of the conference is 'The Apostolic Work'. It is an attempt to show how the principles governing the growth of the early church can be applied to our situation in Chol Chol today.

To emphasise this, on the left-hand side of our founder's portrait is a large map of Paul's missionary journeys, drawn in coloured chalks. Standing under this map and using it to illustrate his points, Doug Milmine gives us one of his inspiring series of talks on the astonishing growth of the early church in Paul's day.

On the right is a similar map, but of our rural centres in Chile today. Standing under this map a number of our people give us up-to-date reports on the development of the work in their particular area. They point to the map to make this clear. For example, Ramón Coñuepán moves us to tears as he tells us how, through his little four-year-old child at the gate of death, the good news of Christ has arrived in power in Pitraco and his church has been established there. Another is Samuel Maripán with his story of how God has brought him back from the very jaws of death during the horrors of the typhus plague that only two months previously has killed so many in his area of Coyimco. The whole programme shows how the same power of God to change lives and to sustain them through every adversity that was seen in apostolic times is very much alive to do the same for us today. All of us now return to our homes rejoicing in the reality of this wonderful truth.

These were, of course, just two outstanding examples of people whose lives had been transformed. Every week dozens more were doing the same in the rural meetings. In Chol Chol itself, Tony was seeing people yield their lives to Christ every week.

One such person was a man called Guillermo Grandón, a notorious criminal. It was known that he had murdered someone during a fierce brawl. He had lost an eye in the fight. Now he, like many others, was impressed with the amazing change in the life of Segundo Morales, the drunkard who had been so wonderfully changed. So Tony visited him and the Lord just opened his heart – there and then he knelt and yielded his life to

Jesus. The next day José Cabezas, another of our leaders, visited him to explain more fully what such a decision really meant. The following Sunday, there he was in the service, rejoicing throughout at what God had done for him. The following morning Tony again slipped in to see Guillermo and found that he was going on excellently. Physically his remaining eye was troubling him but he said, 'Even if the Lord shuts my one remaining eye, I pray he will never shut my mouth from praising him'.

From there Tony went straight to the home of a man called Oñate who had just been released from prison after being fined for being drunk and disorderly. The room was absolutely bare of all furniture except for one little table and some stools. After chatting a while, this man also knelt with his wife and they both accepted the Lord.

It was people like these that were so helped in our monthly and yearly conferences. They needed the support of others to give them strength to resist the taunts and even violence of their old time 'friends' who did everything they could to drag them back into misery.

We also organised similar gatherings in the surrounding countryside, called 'Concentraciones'. These took place in four key areas, roughly according to the points of the compass. They were held in the school holidays, especially the major fiestas. This had a double advantage: first, the people were free to come because it was a holiday; secondly it occupied some that might otherwise have been tempted into a drink shop. Here we baptised lots of people in the nearest river. For those who wished to seek the blessing of God on their sexual relationships we had massed weddings. Surrounded by a great body of well-wishers these were most moving occasions. Our new leaders gave special lectures on appropriate subjects. The singing by such a large number of people, although in the open-air, was truly awe-inspiring. At last we were beginning to win the battle against evil as more and more people's lives were being transformed and strengthened by Christ.

We finished our last year in Chol Chol with our own 'Concentración'. This took place on the 'Isla' in our river. This was a small island, caused by a split in the river that then flowed either side of it. Being in the Southern Hemisphere it was a lovely sunny day just before Christmas! The sixty from our Chol Chol church and locality who were to be baptised were congregated on the island. One by one they entered the water where they were baptised and then crossed over to the riverbank where they joined the huge congregation who waited to greet them, singing the hymns of Zion. This was followed by the reception of the new members and a very solemn Holy Communion service at which they all participated for the first time. We could not have had a more wonderful send off after our four years in Chol Chol.

Yes! There had been perils galore, but we now felt our mission in Chol Chol had been largely accomplished. So when we went on our first home leave, we could safely leave the work in the hands of Bill Flagg. On our return, we moved to Quepe. Here there were facilities for a residential Training Institute with a full-time curriculum. This was Tony's dream and still is; to prepare national workers sufficiently competent to lead the work in the future. Furthermore, we could now include agriculture in the curriculum by using the farm. At last Tony was also able to lecture on elementary veterinary science, just as Bill Flagg had originally envisaged.

CHAPTER SEVENTEEN

Our first home leave

TONY AND I along with our four children were at last together in Temuco in preparation for our journey north to catch the SS 'Reina del Mar' in Valparaiso on our trip back to the UK. Of course the voyage would be quite new to us as we would be returning up the West coast of South America and then through the Panama Canal, whereas when we had come out we had sailed down the East coast to Buenos Aires.

In Valparaiso we were staying with Mrs. Hemans, the daughter of Mr. Sadlier, co-founder with Daddy Wilson of the Chol Chol mission. At the time, the north was suffering a terrible drought. They had to buy a daily supply of water from tankers that came round the streets; this was then stored in buckets and bowls, with the main supply put in the bath. Along comes three-year-old Pattie and, thinking that someone had forgotten to let out the bath water, she kindly pulled the plug. She never was slow to offer a helping hand when needed. Although Mrs. Hemans was very gracious about it, I wished I could have disappeared like the water.

After a relaxing five-week voyage we finally arrival in Plymouth. Once on the jetty, we handed Pattie over the barrier to the two delighted grannies; as she had been born in Chile, they, of course, had not yet seen her and so didn't realise what was in store for them! We then all went together to the home of Tony's parents in Seaton, Devon. Here a letter from head-office was awaiting him with his deputation dates – the interest in hearing about our work was so great that he was booked up

solidly for our six months in the UK. There was also a letter from Australia inviting him to spend three months there on his way back to Chile. Our chance encounter with our Australian friend, Allen Yuell, just before we had left for South America the first time, had born fruit. On returning home, Allen had been appointed chaplain to Howard Mowll, Archbishop of Sydney. It was not long before he had enthused the archbishop with what was going on in Chile. This had led directly to this invitation for Tony to visit there.

Our first duty was to attend the SAMS committee meeting. There we met for the first time the new treasurer, Tony Kimpton and we immediately hit it off. This proved to be a turning point in the history of our work. He had gathered around him a group of successful Christian businessmen who formed the new financial committee for SAMS. Mr. Kimpton told us that from now on they would be able to supply us with all the support we needed. For example we were promised a Unimog, a vehicle suitable for the rough terrain in Chile.

Tony was very concerned about the Quepe farm and was hoping that someone would come forward to take it over when Bill Flagg left. Then he met again a friend from our Slough days, Brian Skinner, who was now a trained agriculturist. That night they had to sleep in the same room. When they went to bed, Tony took the opportunity to explain at some length this need, only to discover when he'd finished that Brain was fast asleep. However, a few days later in the daytime, when Brian was wide-awake, he repeated the message. Eventually, he did join us.

At the end of July we attended the Keswick Convention in the beautiful Lake District. Here we were introduced to a young lady called Kath Clark, but in a rather unusual way. She had become interested in South America and had been given our name in order to find out more. Kath decided to seek us out. It so happened that the new chairman of SAMS, Major Batt, had come to discuss future plans with us. We were just getting down to serious business when the front door bell rang. As nobody answered, I thought the landlady must be out and so went and opened the door. Kath was standing on the doorstep. Thinking that she was the landlady's daughter, I motioned her in and, before she could say anything, hurried back into the meeting and closed the door. Poor Kath was left standing in the hallway, totally perplexed as to what to do. Eventually she plucked up courage and knocked timidly on our door. When she explained the purpose of her visit I was full of apologies; but from this first rather dubious introduction came untold benefits. Not only did she join us in Chile and help us greatly there, but much later, back in the UK, she played a big part in the growth of SAMS.

One of our biggest opportunities was in Oxford. Our old friends, Basil and Stella Gough, had invited us to take part in a short three-day house party where a fine group of earnest young people had gathered. On one of our rambles, Tony had a long talk with David Pytches who seemed very sure that he should go to

Chile. Before we left Oxford, he confirmed to us that he and his wife Mary would be applying to SAMS to join us there, which eventually they did.

A week later we attended our last SAMS committee meeting where it was decided that Tony should return to South America via Australia to raise interest in SAMS. Now we discovered that Aphra Ward, the young secretary in the SAMS office, was not only a first class touch-typist but she was also fluent in Spanish. She offered to join us to help Tony by typing the stencils for his Spanish notes that he would need in the new Institute in Quepe.

The time soon came for Tony to catch his plane for Australia; this was several months before I was due to leave with the kids by boat. It was the first time that he had travelled by air and it was a very long and tiring journey. However, there were a lovely group of people, including Allen Yuell, to welcome him at Sydney airport at 3 o'clock in the morning; that same evening he had to address a distinguished group of SAMS supporters plus bishops, the dean of the cathedral and Archbishop Mowll. Not used to chatting with bishops and archbishops, he felt a little out of his depth; however, they all went out of their way to make him feel comfortable. To top it all, His Grace lent his own chauffeured car to get him home!

Tony was staying in the Yuell's home, on the other side of Sydney Bay. To reach it, he had to travel on the ferry, a delightful trip. As it rounded the tiny headland of the Botanic Gardens it came in under the shadow of the mighty Sydney Harbour Bridge.

From now on Tony was working incessantly, speaking about our work and seeking to encourage support and to interest other young people with the prospect of joining us. He went to churches, meetings of all sorts, schools, spoke on radio and appeared on television. At least it made the days fly by and the time of our being together again seem closer.

Before leaving Australia, he had to visit Melbourne. On the way he flew over the worst of the terrible bush fires that were raging in Australia at that time; it was an awesome sight. Although not on that scale, Tony nearly did serious damage to the cathedral when he was preaching there. As he began to speak, the public address system faded away. This was just the kind of challenge that he relished; he had always prided himself on making himself heard right at the back of the longest church. So he filled his lungs to the full and began to throw his voice to the end of the vast cathedral. That was all right until they suddenly got the amplification restored. The effect was devastating. The whole cathedral rocked to its foundations, the roof nearly collapsed and the whole congregation was left deafened and stunned. Tony went down in history as the pommy who came near to destroying their cathedral.

At the end of his tour, Archbishop Mowll presided over the most wonderful farewell service in Sydney Cathedral. Although his wife lay critically ill, he had insisted on being there in person. Tony was moved to tears as he watched this great man of God, bowed down with his inner grief, determined to give him the very best farewell he could.

From there, he flew to New Zealand and then crossed the Pacific on the Ceramic, a single-class liner, in other words, all first class! So he had a beautiful cabin, with a bathroom to himself. He embarked at 9 p.m. on Friday, November 29th – he awakened next morning to discover that it was STILL Friday, November 29th. They had crossed the DATE LINE!

On the voyage he read a moving book called 'Through Gates of Splendour'. It told of the death of five young Americans in their attempt to reach the much-feared tribe of the Aucas deep in the Ecuadorian jungle. After weeks of careful preparation, flying over the area letting down gifts on the end of a rope, the great day finally arrived when the Indians returned their present by attaching a live parrot to the rope. They now decided that it would be safe to land on the beach of the river in an attempt to make direct contact with them. However, suddenly the Aucas attacked and the five men were speared to death. Tony wondered if by any chance he would meet any of the team that took part in this attempt when he reached Ecuador.

Now came a welcome break from the monotony of the journey. They were approaching Pitcairn Island, famous because of the 'The Mutiny on the Bounty'. Set right in the middle of the Pacific, this was a delightful little craggy island with huts nestling in the folds of the hills. Three good-sized boats, each manned by twelve hefty oarsmen, were awaiting their arrival. Rope ladders were dropped over the side for them; they swarmed up these and all over the ship where they displayed for sale their attractive straw work and carved wooden birds and fish. These people are the descendants of the original mutineers from the Bounty that had all become Christians when they found, read and believed an old Bible. They say that this is now the only port in the world where it is unnecessary to lock your cabin for fear of robberies, which speaks volumes for the sincerity of their faith. They were singing gospel hymns as they left the ship and rowed back to their remote island home.

On his arrival in Panama Tony flew on to Ecuador where he did meet someone directly connected with the five martyrs. Hearing of his intense interest in these events he was invited to stay two weeks in Shell Mera, right in the heart of the Ecuadorian jungle and among many of those who had been involved in this tragic event. As my boat wasn't due to arrive for several weeks he gladly accepted.

He was up early at 4.30 the next morning to catch the bus to Shell Mera. Tony had been puzzled to see how some of the more streetwise passengers climbed up on to the roof of the bus. He soon discovered why – as one of them said, 'On these precipices I can spit for two miles down without hitting anything!' On the top they had a much better chance of jumping off if the worst came to the worst. The bus bulged out on both sides. This meant that Tony's seat, on the precipice side, left him suspended over those dizzy two miles down! Even when he kept his eyes tight shut, he still couldn't blot out the image of that ghastly void gaping beneath him and waiting to swallow him up. Just to aggravate the situation, the driver had taken a tipple too many to bolster his courage!

Suddenly the bus ground to a halt and everyone was ordered off. There before them, the road had disappeared into the crevasse in a mighty landslide. No trouble, they were told, another bus had come to meet them on the other side of the avalanche. Then a team of porters appeared as if from nowhere and, having unloaded the entire luggage from the bus, started off along a slithery path over the landslide. These porters certainly had to be admired; they carried the heavy loads on their backs, supported only by a headband that bore all the weight. Although himself allergic to precipices, Tony meekly decided to follow. Frankly, he didn't have much option, as it was an awfully long walk back to Quito.

Now, right in front of him, one of the bearers slipped and was left half-suspended over the side, only prevented from dropping into the abyss by the weight of his load and the strap around his forehead which was pinning him to the path. His colleagues showed a most bizarre reaction to this disaster. They roared with laughter as they rushed up and heaved him back. To them it was one great joke.

Eventually they reached the bus on the other side and from then on had an uneventful trip into Shell Mera. Here the team received him with every attention. They took him on a number of excursions into the jungle where he got quite a real feeling of their unique life-style. There he also saw the very parrot that the Aucas had attached to the rope as their return gift for the five martyrs.

Then, two days before Christmas, he had the opportunity of a lifetime; Johnny Keenan invited him to come on one of his routine supply flights further into the interior. Tony jumped at the opportunity. In Arajuno, within Auca territory, he met Dr. and Mrs. Tidmarsh; this valiant couple were maintaining an outpost here, serving the small community of Quechua Indians.

Their only defence against a possible Auca attack was a low-current electric fence that encircled the tiny compound. When Tony enquired if they saw anything of the Aucas, they pointed to a stack of 22 spears in the corner of the room; these, they explained, had been removed from one of the Quechuas who imprudently had gone down alone to wash in the river the week before. The Aucas, seeing their chance, had struck again. As a sign of their bitter hostility, they had bound pages torn from one of the martyr's Bibles, to the shafts of the spears.

They then flew on to Shandia where they were greeted by one of the martyr's widows, Betty Elliot. With her were TWO AUCA WOMEN. They had come out of their tribe in search of a younger relative, Dayuma, who had fled years before. Since then she had been teaching Rachel Saint the Auca language; Rachel was the sister of the pilot, Nate Saint, who had died on the beach.

Without realising it at the time, Tony had just participated in what was to become one of the great epics in the history of Christian Missions. When these two Auca women returned to their tribe, Dayuma agreed to go with them. Eventually all three came out again, this time accompanied by seven more Aucas. To everyone's astonishment they said that the Aucas wanted Rachel and Betty to visit them. This they did, along with Betty's four-year-old daughter, Valerie, living among those who had killed their men-folk only three years before. There they taught them about the love of Jesus and many of them eventually came to accept Him for themselves. In God's providence, the sacrifice of the five martyrs had opened the way for two ladies and a baby girl to fulfil their hopes.

Back in Shell Mera it seemed strange to be celebrating Christmas with the full 'Yankie' dinner of turkey and cranberry jelly in the middle of the Ecuadorian jungle. After dinner two of the younger boys tried out their new boxing gloves on each other which did seem rather an odd way of expressing 'peace on earth and goodwill towards men'! However, with all these amazing experiences to share with me, Tony couldn't wait to get to the coast where he waited impatiently for my arrival with the children on the 'Reina del Mar'.

CHAPTER EIGHTEEN

Together again

EARLY IN December, 1957, it was time for me and the children to say goodbye to our dear parents and friends, as we were due to return to Chile again. Tony was on his way back from Australia and travelling to South America across the Pacific; I would be embarking on the 'Reina del Mar' in Liverpool with the four children and would be travelling in the opposite direction across the Atlantic. We planned to meet up off the coast of Ecuador in about four weeks time.

I was in Hove with my parents and just finishing packing, ready to leave the next day, when I suddenly got a wire from SAMS office telling me to travel up to London that same night. Apparently, the fog was so thick in London that if we left it until tomorrow we would miss the boat train for Liverpool. What a scramble! I threw the last-minute things in the cases, Daddy got a taxi and, after emotional hugs and goodbyes, we set off for Brighton Station and eventually arrived at Waterloo. We had been booked into the St Pancreas Station Hotel so we still had to cross London to get there. All five of us piled into a taxi; along with our bags it didn't leave much space for us. The message had been right; the fog was so thick that a man with a flaming torch had to walk in front of our taxi all the way to St Pancreas Station. It was a huge pea-souper!

After what seemed like an eternity, we finally arrived at St Pancreas Station Hotel. There we had a snack and then, all in one room, fell into bed exhausted. I hardly slept because I was so afraid that I wouldn't wake up in time to catch the early boat train for Liverpool next morning. During breakfast, I happened to spot the headlines of an early morning newspaper that was lying there. This read, 'FATAL TRAIN CRASH'. To my great concern I read that there had been a terrible crash on the later train that we had originally planned to take and that a number of people had been killed or injured. I just hoped that Tony wouldn't hear this awful news and think that we had been on the train as intended. The problem was that I now had no means of contacting him until we actually met up again.

In Liverpool, we boarded our now familiar 'Reina del Mar'. Here we also met up with Aphra Ward, the young bi-lingual secretary who was joining us to work with Tony in the new Quepe Institute. Together we hurried to our large cabin for six; we were to share this with Aphra until we met up with Tony in Ecuador. The first two days of the voyage were damp and cold, not at all pleasant; but when we got to Coruña in Spain the weather changed for the better and we were able to go ashore. So we all took a bus to the beach; the children now began to relax as they really enjoyed themselves there.

As on our previous journey out, we passed the usual ports and then struck out across the Atlantic. Now the excitement began. Ominous announcements were being made over the radio of a great storm approaching. We realised the urgency of these reports as the captain kept changing direction in an attempt to avoid it. We heard that even the 'Queen Mary' had turned back and taken refuge in port. Everyone was discussing the tragic fate of the 'Pamir', one of the last four-masted tall-ships, which had recently gone down with all hands on board in a similar ferocious storm.

They now battened down all our hatches and locked the doors and portholes. Unfortunately, we had the misfortune to be in a cabin directly under the deck where the anchor was; this caused a shattering noise every time the ship rolled from side to side. In the cabin next to ours, there was a young mother travelling with her baby and toddler to join her husband in Rio. In the night her porthole burst open and the cabin was flooded.

The members of the crew were marvellous and she was quickly moved to another cabin. We also did what we could to help and comfort her.

The cook was thrown on top of the hot stove where he got badly burnt and broke his arm; so we had cold food. Any table that slid across the floor was smashed to matchwood. Much of the crockery was also broken and a number of passengers injured. The towering waves kept crashing over our liner; one moment all would be light, the next, pitch darkness as these broke over us.

What made it worse was that the ship's stabilisers had both been broken. Consequently, nearly everyone on board was sick. Aphra, a seasoned sailor, was very proud of the fact that on all her previous voyages to South America and back, she had never been seasick. This time she was!

A group of nuns from Portugal were huddled together in the lounge in absolute misery. I felt so sorry for them as their row of chairs kept sliding across the floor and back again with each toss and roll of the boat. Our Rosemary had her finger crushed in the toilet door, as it slammed closed; we had to go to the hospital to have the nail removed, her finger splinted and her arm put in a sling.

After five days the storm started to abate and we were at last able to open the hatches once more. Now an urgent message came over the radio, 'Could we receive an injured sailor in our hospital from a boat nearby?' We all watched with bated breath as the boat drew as near as it could and they slung over a line and pulled the injured man inch by inch across the chasm on a stretcher. Rosemary was especially concerned about this as she could actually see the agony on his face; from then on she prayed for him each night.

Eventually calm was restored. We had been driven far off course to the north so the captain made for the nearest haven which was the beautiful island of Bermuda. The approach was so tranquil nothing could have been more different from the storm through which we had just passed. The sea was turquoise and transparently clear; the sand, coral-pink and the grass and vegetation fresh green. Here, the ship was able to restock and to repair most of the damage.

When we got ashore, we could hardly walk; after the heaving of the boat we were reeling about as if drunk. Terry, with his first step, fell flat on his back! The highlight for us was the unspoilt beauty of the place. Also, because of its English heritage, we were able to find a lovely café where we could have a gorgeous cup of hot English tea with fresh milk and munch away happily at the delicious sandwiches.

When we set sail again there was another big event – the baptism of a little baby that had been born in the storm. A nice Dutch Roman Catholic priest called Gerald took the service. Everyone gathered on the deck to witness the ceremony where the ship's bell was used as the font. Afterwards, the baby was given a certificate for free travel for life on the ship, as is the custom on these rare occasions. We have a nice photograph of the event and there, right at the front of the crowd, taking in everything that went on was – you guess who – Rosemary, with her arm still in a sling, and Hilary.

When, after our evening meal we returned to our cabin, we were surprised to find the ship's doctor and his nurse talking to the children. Pattie had had a slight ear infection and the doctor was checking on this. But now Pattie was entertaining them with her little picture Bible. She was explaining graphically the story of the little lamb that got lost and was then found. They seemed quite touched by her earnestness. The next night they were there again, this time with the injured seaman who had been saved from the other boat. He was a lot better although his arm, like Rosemary's, was still in a sling. They were two injured warriors together! 'Oh! Good!' said Rosemary, 'I've been praying for you ever since I saw you being pulled from the other boat'. With a nice smile and evident sincerity he replied, 'Thank you very much. Your prayers for me were certainly answered.' Later, at one of the lunch times, Rosemary and this injured sailor were suddenly called out to the front, both of them with their arms in a sling. They were each solemnly presented with one of the ship's silver spoons as an award for bravery.

From Bermuda we sailed to Havana, the capital of the island of Cuba. Aphra was especially keen to go ashore as it was Spanish speaking and she was fluent in Spanish. I wasn't keen. However, rather than let her go alone, I decided to accompany her. The port was absolutely filthy and simply stank; furthermore it was very hot, humid and sinister. We wandered around a bit but there was nothing interesting near. Then we saw an ice-cream parlour so we went in. At the counter there were two men to whom Aphra immediately got chatting, which made me a bit nervous. They began talking about the boat when one of them said, 'Oh! We're sailing on her tomorrow. What time does she sail?' This made me really suspicious and so I gave Aphra a kick under the table and hissed, 'If they were sailing on her they would know the time of sailing'. When we had finished our ice-creams we left and went back to the boat.

Next morning at sea we heard that Fidel Castro had entered Havana and that Batista had been deposed. Now we realised why so many Cubans had visited the ship ostensibly to see people off but had stayed on board when the ship sailed with just the clothes they stood up in. Among these, we saw the two fellows that we'd spoken to the day before. I think our captain allowed this extraordinary breach of procedure, as he must have known what was coming – as we all heard later, there was a terrible blood-bath.

We celebrated Christmas towards the end of our voyage but, without Tony, it wasn't the same. As we've seen, but unknown to us at the time, he was celebrating in Shell Mera in the heart of the Ecuadorian jungle.

Now, as we approached the coast of Ecuador our four little children careered from stern to bow, from port to starboard, from crow's nest to the bowels of the vessel, yelping with excitement, 'Daddy's coming, Daddy's coming'. By now the whole passenger list and crew were buzzing with expectation too. When at last they spotted the tiny launch setting out from the jetty, their squeals of 'There's Daddy, there's Daddy' reached a new peak of intensity. The whole of cabin and first class swarmed to the rails and the vessel listed ominously to port as everyone strained to get a glimpse of him to see what this 'Daddy' could be like.

Once he climbed on deck, the welcome he received was awesome. The children climbed all over him and hung on to him wherever he went. Then we pulled two large tables together and all our friends joined us for a special tea with a huge welcome cake that the ship's company had made. Mind you, Tony had a flying start because most of the crew remembered him from our voyage home the year before and seemed genuinely to be looking forward to seeing him again. Now we just couldn't stop talking as we exchanged all the news of what had happened to us on our respective journeys since we had parted.

On New Year's Day we arrived in Callao. Here Mr. Twentyman, the general secretary of the Bible Society in Peru, met us. He kindly took us for a tour of Lima. We hadn't realised before what a beautiful city it was. After a lovely lunch, Tony entertained the kids with their roller skates so that Aphra and I could have a peaceful chat with our hosts. Mr. Twentyman then drove us back to the boat.

As we were in port for the second day, Tony and I went ashore again for a little while and sat in the plaza by the side of the docks. It was interesting to think that the Kon-Tiki expedition had left from this spot. By a coincidence we also bumped into the doctor from St. Mark's college who had been Tony's opponent at deck tennis on our home-ward journey the year before.

Two day's later we arrived in Chile again and were greeted by the strong smell of pelican droppings! Tony and I stayed aboard as Aphra kindly took Terry ashore in Arica. They had to take the launch and with the heavy swell it was quite scary. In Antofogasta Tony, Aphra and I went ashore and attended the Sunday morning service in a little chapel. After, as we were walking down the street, we bumped into Gerald, the Dutch Roman Catholic priest from the boat; he was the one who had officiated at the baptism of the baby after the storm. I was so glad, because I had wanted him to meet Tony so we invited him out to lunch and for three hours had a grand talk together about the things of God.

Two days later we arrived back in Valparaiso. Here we met Marion Garvin. This was significant as she was later to marry Ian Morrison and they became one of the most beautiful couples that it has ever been our privilege to know. Two days later we were back in Temuco where, among others, Ian Morrison and all the Milmines were on the platform to welcome us. Tony's entry in his diary was 'Oh what pure joy to be back!'

CHAPTER NINETEEN

On the banks of the River Quepe

ON OUR return from the UK we moved to the Quepe farm to set up the new Leadership and Agricultural Training Institute there. We were now about twenty miles from Chol Chol and ten from Temuco. On a clear day to the East we could just make out the snow-capped peaks of the Andes, two of which, Llaima and Villarica were active volcanoes.

Technically speaking, Quepe was not the correct name for our farmland. We always referred to it as such among ourselves because the nearby village, with its modest railway station, was called Quepe. Also it seemed a convenient name, as the River Quepe flowed through it, dividing it into two. The official name, however, was Maquehue-Pelal, but that was a bit of a mouthful! On the North of the river was Maquehue (Ma-kay-way), with the cottage hospital-cum-dispensary, from which a path ran through an orchard to the church. On the South was Pelal with the farmhouse, farm shop, school and flourmill. It could hardly have been more different from Chol Chol, it was so quiet and peaceful.

The River Quepe was beautiful, skirted by high banks that were covered with green bamboo and trees. In the earlier days, a ferry had connected the two sides, but in our time we had the advantage of quite a long wooden suspension bridge. This swayed alarmingly, especially when crossing on horseback or in a vehicle; even worse when herding cattle! As there was a high drop into the river, this could be quite scary. We moved to our new work on these beautiful banks of the River Quepe in mid-February 1958.

With the start of the new academic year, the three girls went to our local mission school. Rosemary was now nine years old, Hilary seven and Pattie five. We had to leave Terry in Temuco so that he could move up to secondary school, as he was now thirteen. For me, this was quite a wrench as it was the first time we had been separated.

The girls simply loved Quepe, especially all the wildlife. One day I heard a shrill, ear-splitting whistle as Rosemary came running in with her hands cupped around the noise. Opening her hands, she gasped, 'Look what's fallen out of the barn roof. It hasn't got a Mummy, so we must feed it, mustn't we?' I realised that it was a baby rat, but it certainly didn't look like one. To me it looked just like a miniature hippopotamus – grey-pink skin, no hair, bulging sealed eyes and a deep pink cavernous mouth where all the sound was coming from. 'Mummy, we've just got to look after it or it will die' I was requested. 'He'll need milk all through the night. I'm just going to get a box with some cotton wool to keep it in.' When she returned she solemnly placed it in the draw of our bedside table, on the grounds that she was sure she wouldn't wake up for the half-hourly feeding times. My heart sank, but weakly I obeyed and found a pen filler and warm milk.

On my first effort, I half drowned the poor thing, but at least it seemed to silence it for half an hour. However, the thought of sleeping with this all night; not to mention what my dear husband would have to say about it, was just too much for me. I'm afraid, after all the kids were in bed, I took the cowardly way out. I crept down to Don Carmelo, our odd-job man, and asked him please to deal with it. I felt murderous but frankly it was either the poor little rat's funeral or mine, if I'd asked Tony to sleep with that for a week or two! In the morning, reluctantly, Rosemary accepted this and so we held a solemn funeral in our garden. From then on I always kept a small bottle of chloroform by me for any other emergencies of a similar kind that the children brought me. Some we saved and a few, like this poor little chap, we just had to lose. So this funeral was the start of what became their animal cemetery as the row of graves lengthened with the demise of other pets.

Hilary was also in her element in Quepe, where the quietness of the countryside and river suited her down to the ground. Also she loved the local people. She was especially fond of two little Mapuche girls called Nena and Ellie Quiñenao. They were real friends and all keen members of our Sunday School. On one occasion we discovered by chance that they had decided to have a Communion Service of their own. They had got some bread and juice from somewhere and Hilary had been chosen to officiate. Although Pattie was two years younger she was let in on sufferance but we were too old and so were not invited to participate. However, we could tell from her report of the event that they did this extremely seriously. One of our colleagues was offended when she learned what had happened; we couldn't help thinking that the Lord would have been very pleased at the sincerity and reverence of these little children.

Hilary loved all God's creatures. They held a special place in her heart and she was always concerned for every aspect of their well being. On one terrible night, with a dreadful storm blowing, she had just been praying for all the birds, rabbits, rats and mice in the district when she suddenly asked me solicitously, 'Mummy, where do all de little dicky-birds and bunny rabbits go in all de rain?' Only after the most detailed description of their nests and burrows did she eventually snuggle down contentedly and go off to sleep herself, happy in the knowledge that they were all as cosy as she was.

As we lived in the country, our food was extremely basic; it always caused quite a stir when we heard that visitors were coming from Britain. We were now expecting an important member of our London committee so I sent Hilary over to Sra. Quiñenao with a string bag to buy a chicken. Off she went and returned happily with a hen. 'Mummy' she said, 'Her name is Mary and I've told her that she's got nothing to worry about. She'll be quite safe with us and she's going to lay us an egg every day!' So we had beans for lunch and so did our distinguished visitor. For her part, Mary kept her side of the bargain and laid us an egg nearly every day, until at a ripe old age she died a natural death.

Pattie continued to get up to her usual pranks. I had to be on the watch all the time as when one of the students came to ask me, 'Do you know that your little girl is in the outhouse cutting her hair off?' I rushed over in time to find that Pattie had already successfully cropped off one side of her beautiful shoulder-length golden hair and was just about to start on the second side. She looked for all the world like an early version of a punk. Now my problem was how to cut just enough off the other side to make her look reasonably presentable. Each morning when I saw her, it was a fresh shock to me. I wondered if I would ever get over her new hairstyle; but gradually I got used to it.

In spite of these burdens of motherhood, both Tony and I also loved the life in Quepe. Even when we were still in Chol Chol we had taken part in a number of activities there that made us aware of the great potential especially of the farm if rightly developed and used. For example, we had taken part in a House Party in Quepe for young anglo-chileans drawn from the big cities. On this occasion, we had loads of activities such as games, horse riding, swimming, treasure hunts etc. To add a bit of spice to the programme, Tony and Doug decided to play a prank on the young people. They found an old torch with changing coloured lights. When it was dark, with everyone in bed, Tony wrapped himself in a sheet and, helped by Doug's shoves from behind, managed to scramble on top of the veranda roof, right outside the young people's dormitories.

This white-clad ghostlike figure appeared outside the girls' window; as the grimacing face went white, red and green in turns, the girls' screams were enough to raise the dead. Outside the boys' window the ghost act was repeated. Suddenly Doug gave a yell from below, 'Look out, Tony!' Glancing round, Tony found himself looking down the barrel of a loaded revolver. Our

very elderly Mapuche retainer, Don Carmelo, startled from sleep by the screams, had come to investigate. Seeing the 'ghost', he decided to shoot it. Tony's reaction was understandably instantaneous; just in time, he rolled down the roof and on to the ground. We couldn't help wondering what the headlines of the papers would have been had he failed to do so – 'Missionary shot while attempting to climb into girls' dormitory at night'.

Several nights later Tony and I had the weirdest experience. We had just switched off the light and were settling down in bed, when something rattled close to Tony's ear and then actually brushed across his face. Thinking one of the youngsters must be getting his own back for the ghost episode, Tony leapt out of bed and switched on the light, but there was nobody in the room. As the door was shut, there didn't seem to be any way in which someone could have got in. Mystified, he locked the door and bolted the window, confident that this would fix it. Once more he got back into bed and switched off the light. Incredibly, after a while the same thing happened again. Once more he switched on the light only to find that there was no one in the room. Not believing in ghosts ourselves, we decided to try to ignore it, sure that the prankster would tell us his or her secret in the morning.

Next morning, I carefully prepared Tony to go down to breakfast. I rubbed Talcum Powder into his hair to make it prematurely grey, I blackened one of his eyes and, to finish the effect, I draped an empty picture frame around his neck. In this state he tottered down stairs and, groaning loudly, joined the group. However, to our surprise the joke seemed to fall flat; no one owned up to the prank. Only later in the day did our dear friend Bill Flagg confess that he had done it! Hearing the scary stories of the youngsters about the ghost and guessing who was the real culprit, he had decided to get his revenge on their behalf. Knowing the geography of the farmhouse so well, he knew that he could get up into the loft and from there loosen the boards of the bedroom ceiling enough to lower a bunch of dried seaweed on a cord. Before we could switch on the lights he had been able to pull it up again and replace the board. So at last the mystery was solved.

In spite of (or perhaps because of) all these shenanigans, the house party was a tremendous success. Several of the youngsters became our closest allies. One young lad called Tomasello, when describing what he had seen on the roof, said, with his eyes popping out of his head, 'First it was white, then it was green, then it was red. It was terrible'. But he and his wife, Alicia, both now medical doctors, are loyal members of Terry's church in Viña del Mar.

I have a few further recollections of events on the banks of the River Quepe. One of these took place in a small house at the very entrance to the suspension bridge. This was the home of the Paredes family, faithful members of our church. Our nurse, Helen Bridge, had been attending the Granny but sadly she had died. I had such happy memories of visiting her and admired her small garden and flowers that she tended with such care. Now I was helping to prepare her body for burial. As this was the first time I had helped in this capacity I found it a bit creepy. Suddenly as Helen pulled her into a sitting position to wash her back, the body emitted a long, eerie groan as the air was forcibly exhaled from her lungs. My hair stood on end! For a moment I thought the poor dear wasn't really dead. Sadly it was not to be and we had the funeral to celebrate her life in our little Quepe church.

The other incident on the banks of the River Quepe occurred some time later when Nurse Shirley Goodwin had replaced Helen. An anxious father from the other side of the river came to ask if I could go to help his wife who was in labour. He'd been to get Shirley but had been told that she had gone to the hospital in Temuco with an emergency case. I am not a trained nurse, far less a midwife, but having had four children of my own I suppose by now I knew a thing or two! Thinking Shirley would soon be back, I agreed to go; after all, I thought, at least I could talk to her, rub her back and comfort her with what was to be her first baby. So we hurried over the suspension bridge to their hut. I found the mother lying on her bed in a tiny room. It was so small that there was hardly space to move. There I continued helping her for a couple of hours.

By now it was dark, so one of our colleagues came over to see what had happened to me. Finding me with only a Nestle's Milk tin lamp for light, she offered to go back to get a Tilly lamp. Before she could return with this, baby decided to turn up. It was a lovely, healthy little girl.

Now I had to deal with the placenta; this I carefully put in a bowl so that Shirley could check it when she arrived. I was a bit worried about how to tie the cord until I spotted some strips of rags hanging by some string. With these I double tied the cord to be on the safe side. I knew Shirley would attend to it when she returned. Having made them comfortable I now went home.

The next day, Shirley was still not back, so at 8 a.m. I crossed the suspension bridge again to see how my two patients, Mum and babe, were. From the distance the first thing I saw was a group of men congregated outside. My heart sank. 'Oh! No! Surely they aren't making a coffin' I thought. However, as I got closer I could see that they had just killed a sheep. They welcomed me and said that the mother and baby were fine.

While I was talking to the mother, and washing the babe, in they walked with an enamel plate on which was a good serving of steamy sheep's blood; to my horror they offered this to me as a reward for my services; it was considered to be the ultimate delicacy. We had always accepted everything we were offered, but at 8 a.m. in the morning steamy blood was just too much for me. I heaved at the thought. Offering up a quick prayer for deliverance, the Lord gave me a way of escape. I said 'Ah! That's just what the mother needs for strength. But I would appreciate a maté'. However, it was nearly as bad watching her slurping down the congealed blood. Shirley came back and, after checking, pronounced everything to be fine.

CHAPTER TWENTY

The Quepe Training Institute

NOW THAT we had settled into the life at Quepe, we began to implement our plans for establishing a Training Institute there. After the success of the weekly Leaders' Training Course in Chol Chol, we felt that it was time to build on this foundation with something more substantial. The new Institute would be an advance on our lectures in Chol Chol that had been once a week; this would be a full-time Residential Leadership Training Institute with three lectures a day, five days a week, for a whole year. It would also include a very full agricultural programme in its curriculum. Now Tony could put his veterinary knowledge to use by lecturing on basic animal diseases, their prevention and cure; even simple information on animal obstetrics.

His days were mainly taken up with preparing lectures with the intention of training national workers to take over the pastoral work of the church, much as he had done in Chol Chol. Using his material from the Chol Chol courses, he set these out in printed form so that each student could have their copy to take back to their homes. Our other colleagues also lectured on their specialist subjects as and when they were available. You may also remember how, while we were in England, I had closed the door in the face of a girl who had come to visit us during the Keswick convention! Undeterred, Kath Clark had eventually joined us as a principal lecturer in the Institute. Our other new colleague, Aphra Ward, typed out all these notes on stencils; then she duplicated these on the new machine we had brought out from the UK.

As most of the Mapuches lived off their smallholdings we decided that the heart of their agricultural training would be to look after a 'Model Smallholding'. They could then put into practice some of the latest scientific advances as they were taught to them.

The Institute opened its doors for classes on our Wedding Anniversary, April 11th 1958. A number of local students came in daily to attend the classes; those who came from afar, for example from the Chol Chol area, lived in as residents. For these, we devised what we called our 'Rotation System'. Each rural centre was invited to send one or two of their members to the Institute for a year's training. While they were away from home, the other members looked after their smallholding for them. The following year, when they had returned home, they would then look after the land of two more students, to allow them to study, and so on. Of course, those who returned home were immediately able to put into practice all that they had learned, in improving their own land and animal care. But just as importantly, they were now able to do the same for the smallholdings they were attending for the new students, to give them a flying start. After several years, the benefits were considerable.

The time-table was quite intensive:

Mornings: Three lectures on leadership training, an hour each.

Afternoons: Practical work on the farm or buildings, along with lectures on agriculture.

Evenings: Tutorials to discuss the printed notes on the morning's subjects.

Sundays: Afternoon visitation of the surrounding rural centres to put into practice the new leadership skills that they had acquired.

The Institute was self-supporting. The students not only got excellent practical work on the farm but what they produced was used to feed them; surpluses were sold to pay for the expenses of their tuition such as text books, printed notes, etc. There must have been between fifteen and twenty students, the number varying as some only attended special classes. There was a good representation from the Chol Chol region as well as from the Quepe and Temuco areas.

While we were in England, Reg Bartle and his wife Thelma had been holding the fort in Quepe. This magnificent new couple had joined us just before we had left for our first home leave. Reg had faithfully visited the people in the Quepe area and among his many contacts was the Mena family in Mahuidache. As a result, Alberto Mena and his sister Angelina had become Christians and had asked him to arrange for services to be held in their modest family home. They were two of our first students to enrol. While Alberto worked for his keep with the other male students on the farm, she lived in our home and helped me with the children and we all became very fond of her. Later, when we were caught in the big earthquake, Angelina was a tower of strength.

Naturally, for their weekend practical work, they and their fellow students would often visit their small but growing congregation in Mahuidache. So we now began to form a plan to establish them in their own church building. After some serious financial setbacks, at last the farm was beginning to prosper. As the students were contributing to this development with their afternoon work, Tony and his staff felt that some of the profits should be ploughed back into their community. An obvious first candidate to benefit was the new church in Mahuidache. Some of the students were good carpenters and all were only too willing to help in the construction. So plans were drawn up for a miniature version of our central church in Quepe, with its small bell-tower over the entrance door.

Eventually we moved into the centre in Temuco where we were in a better position to acquire good quality wood at a reasonable price; and so the building commenced. It so happened that over this period our home committee had sent out a professional photographer to make a film of all that was going on. Naturally, he covered the building of this church in full. Unfortunately, for some reason he badly under-exposed this part of the film and so had to reject it. We got permission to use these sections, along with all the other rejects, and carefully pieced them together to make a second film, entitled 'The Wind of God'. As we often continued with the construction well after dark we used these under-exposed sections to represent these night scenes; they really did look most convincing. This film was widely circulated, even reaching Tony's friends in Australia, to their great delight.

As one of our last tasks before returning on our second home leave we were able to attend the festivities celebrating the opening of this new church and to install Alberto as the lay pastor; his right-hand helper was, of course, my dear Angelina. The Institute was beginning to yield fine results.

Pedro Ancán, a Mapuche, was a student with special learning difficulties as he could scarcely read or write although he clearly was very intelligent. In spite of these disabilities, his Mission had enrolled him in the more advanced Christian and Missionary Alliance Seminary in Temuco. Sadly, he was totally out of his depth. So they asked us if we would be willing to take him on. It was our biggest academic challenge yet, because it would be difficult to accommodate him in our classes without jeopardising the progress of the others, as these did at least have the basic literacy skills. However, we felt we should take up this challenge.

The first thing was to gain the co-operation of the other students. We explained to them that this was a part of their own training; to develop the patience necessary to help others less fortunate than themselves. They rose to the occasion. Pedro became very popular for his out-going personality and commitment to improving himself. Because of his difficulty in writing, we made special provision for him, and whenever possible substituted oral testing for a written exam. The improvement in his results was then dramatic, showing that he certainly didn't lack ability, only the advantage of a basic education.

Following his year in our Institute he had improved so much that the Alliance Seminary agreed to give him another chance. Continuing with our method of testing, he did very well. On graduating, he became a popular producer on a local Christian radio station, reaching many appreciative listeners.

Perhaps the most talented and disciplined student that we had was a young disabled Chilean lad. Poor Bernardo Avila was totally incapacitated; his legs were just twigs, crossed tightly over each other and completely useless; his arms and hands were much the same. He had to lie permanently on his back in a half-moon position, even when reading and writing and yet he never complained. His fellow students looked after him extremely well, washing and dressing him. To give him some mobility, they made him a little wooden cart and in this they wheeled him around wherever they went.

He was brilliant with all his studies. In fact he was so outstanding that for the second year we appointed him tutor and as such he excelled and became a permanent junior member of staff. Our whole idea was to teach the students to a standard where they in turn could teach others also. In Bernardo, this objective was more than fulfilled.

To give him a treat, Doug Milmine drove him up to Santiago to see the sites of the capital. He put his little cart in the back of his long-bodied Land Rover, and propped him up as much as he could by his side on the front seat. It was a lovely day and Bernardo, who had never had a long journey like this through the glorious Chilean countryside, was absolutely entranced. He ooohd and aaaahd non-stop. 'So this is my country' he gasped. 'I had no idea it was so beautiful.'

The next day, Doug drove him through the city and down to the presidential palace, 'La Moneda'. As they entered the precincts, the carabinero on guard in his impeccable uniform and highly-polished jackboots checked them in. He greeted Bernardo with a kindly smile. Once inside, Bernardo watched wide-eyed the precision marching at the changing of the guard, led by the brilliant brass band.

When the time came to leave, Doug had to drag the poor lad away! On the way out, they passed again the same carabinero who had checked them in. This time he stopped them and enquired solicitously of Bernardo, 'I'm so sorry to see you like that. Did you have a serious accident or something?' 'Please don't be sorry for me' he replied brightly, 'I'm a Christian and I've got the Lord Jesus Christ in my heart to help me. I'm very happy and quite all right'. The guard was deeply moved by his remarkable courage.

Later, Bernardo married one of our missionary nurses who immigrated with him to Australia; there she was able to arrange for his legs to be broken and straightened. Although he was still unable to walk, this meant that he could now be seated comfortably in a wheel chair. In Australia, he took up the unusual hobby of collecting caps! Because of this he became quite a personality on television and radio, speaking on his hobby. As he became widely known, people would send him caps of all shapes, sizes and colours from all over Australia.

Years later, when Terry was visiting Australia and had just alighted from his plane in Sydney airport, he heard a shrill voice, from one side of the terminal to the other, greeted him, 'Terryyyyy!' It was Bernardo who zipped in and out of the astonished crowd with his ultramodern, self-propelled wheelchair that he drove with the speed and dexterity of a racing driver. So our one-time Institute student, speaking in Spanish with a strong Australian accent, now had a great time reminiscing with Terry on all the escapades that he and his fellow students had got up to in those far-off days on the banks of the River Quepe.

Delighted with the effects of the methods of our Quepe Institute on Pedro Ancán, the following year the Alliance Mission in Temuco asked Tony if he would repeat his course on the Pentateuch in their seminary. As the students were much more advanced, Tony had to work hard to modify his notes accordingly, honing and refining his material. Many years later, he discovered to his surprise that there had been such a demand for these notes that they had published them in book form!

With hindsight, we now realise that the period in the Quepe Institute had an importance far beyond the walls of that Institute. The reason for this was that these notes later provided the fertile source material for the self-instructional 'Study by Extension for All Nations' courses that were developed when we got to Tucumán, in Argentina, in the early seventies. These courses, known as SEAN (pronounced Say-An), have had an amazing spread and effect throughout the world, especially among those previously deprived of adequate education. But in some measure the seeds for this were sown in these humble beginnings in Chol Chol and Quepe.

CHAPTER TWENTY-ONE

Parental joys and anguish

UP TO now we had had all four of our babies delivered at home, either in England or Chile. We wanted the same for our fifth with Muriel Parrott in attendance as she had been with Pattie in Chol Chol. So from Quepe we moved temporarily into our centre in Temuco as this would be easier and quicker for her to get to us. A few days earlier than expected, I woke up at midnight and labour had started. Tony was visiting out in Quepe and miles away; there was no way in which Muriel could have got there in time from Chol Chol. So I phoned the doctor and he told me to go round the corner to the clinic and he would come. As there was no point in waking everyone up, I left a note on the bed to say where I was. Then I popped my overcoat over my nightie, put the things for baby into the carrycot and walked round to the clinic. All went well and baby Jonathan (or Jonnie for short) was born at 6.30 a.m., all ten and a half pounds of him. At 7.30 our other children, Terry, Rosemary, Hilary and Pattie, having read my note on the bed, raced round, much to the amusement of the nurses. Terry in particular was wreathed in smiles because at last he had got his brother. It was the 15th March, 1959.

Aphra Ward kindly agreed to go out to Quepe to give Tony the good news and bring him back to celebrate with the others. When she arrived, in her excitement she blurted out to Tony, 'Congratulations, you've got two boys', meaning Terry and the new baby. Tony, however, thinking she meant that we'd had twins, returned to Temuco floating on air! However, when he found that his 'twins' was a ten-pound bouncer he was more than

147

satisfied. Better still, both Jonnie and I were so well that I was allowed home the next day and so we were able to return to Quepe.

Our joy over Jonnie's birth was rudely interrupted. I was putting Hilary and Pattie to bed and we had just finished our prayers when I heard a vehicle draw up outside. As I went down to answer the door a strange sense of foreboding passed over me. It was Aphra, who had driven out this time to break the appalling news that Rosemary had been involved in a serious accident. She was now living in Temuco with Kath and Aphra in order to attend secondary school and so was in hospital there. I grabbed the laundry basket, threw in Jonnie's nappies and baby things and popped him in on top. I then told the girls that Rosemary had been hurt and that we were going to see how she was; we had another little prayer together before we left them in the safe hands of our home help. We drove into Temuco through an awful storm and went straight to the hospital. Rosemary was in the very room where I had been when I had had my operation for my gall bladder. The room was crowded with people, the schoolteachers that had seen the accident and many other missionary friends who had come to help.

We took one look at Rosemary and saw immediately how extremely serious it was. One side of her face and body was paralysed while the other was convulsed by epileptic spasms. Those present told us what had happened. Apparently a young fellow, completely drunk, had been tearing down the street in a big car just as the children were coming out of school. A group of girls ran over the road but Rosemary stayed on the pavement. On swerving to avoid the group, he mounted the pavement and sent Rosemary flying. She received a terrible blow on one side of her head from the speeding car while the other side of her head struck the road violently as she fell. She was picked up unconscious and raced to the hospital. We thanked all our friends for their support but asked if now we could please be left quietly alone. To us the case seemed hopeless and the doctor who came in felt the same. He told us that the only hope for her was to have brain surgery in Santiago but she wouldn't stand up to the journey in an ambulance and no available planes would fly because of the ferocity of the storm.

He did add, however, that if we would agree to the risk, in the last resort he would be willing to open her skull in an attempt to lessen the pressure on her brain as he had done this once before in an emergency. However, as a preliminary step he tried to relieve some of the pressure on her brain by drawing off quite a quantity of fluid and blood from her spine with a lumbar puncture.

Tony and I sat with her all through the night and the doctor kindly kept coming in and out to check her reflexes and to see if he could get any response on her paralysed side. In the early hours, he got a slight reaction as she moved her foot a fraction. The epileptic spasms had slightly eased also. This gave us a ray of hope. Later the next day, she began to stir and to our joy, although apparently still unconscious she recognised Tony's voice and fumbled for his hand and kissed it. From then on she gradually regained consciousness.

The drunken lad who had caused the accident had been driving his father's car. His father was the local bank manager and his poor mother actually worked in the hospital, and every spare minute sat outside Rosemary's door desperate to learn of any improvement in her condition. Our hearts grieved for her as we thought of all she must be going through.

Everyone presumed we would sue the boy's family. Instead we decided that Tony would have a serious talk with him. He pointed out that it was only through God's grace and in answer to all our prayers that Rosemary had not died and that he had not been put in prison for manslaughter. He urged him to take on board the lesson, to abandon excessive alcohol and to change his life by seeking Christ's forgiveness and help.

Eventually the doctor let us take Rosemary home to Quepe. After about a month she seemed a lot better, the only sign left was that she dragged one foot and her pupil was dilated. However, instead of being the usual bubbly extravert, for a while she was more inclined to withdraw into herself and became more unpredictable. Gradually she recovered and happily is now her old, cheerful self again.

No sooner had we begun to get over the shock of Rosemary's accident than another storm burst over us, just as bad. After Jonnie's safe delivery, he had developed into a lovely, healthy, happy baby. Then, when he was five months old and I was bathing him, I suddenly noticed a lump at the back of his shoulder that I thought was odd. I took him in to Tony who palpated it and said that he felt we should take him into Temuco to check. The doctor thought that it was probably a lipoma (fatty tumour) and told us to keep an eye on it.

In ten days time it was double the size and spreading. We went back and our doctor consulted with several of his colleagues in the hospital; that night they operated on him. They were shocked to find that the tumour had long roots penetrating right into his spine. They couldn't remove any more or he would have been paralysed.

The biopsy revealed what in our hearts we already knew; it was malignant. He got over the operation very quickly and seemed so fit that when I went for his check-up with the doctor I was becoming more optimistic. Gravely, the doctor had to warn me, 'Señora, you MUST NOT have any hope or you will only be more hurt; I fear that a malignant tumour on such a young baby will grow much more quickly than on an adult'.

But we and all our friends kept praying. One afternoon, after we got back to Quepe, three Mapuche Christians came in on horseback to visit us; they had heard the news about Jonnie and asked if they could pray for him. We were deeply moved at their faith, love and concern and, of course, gratefully accepted. Indeed, as they heard the news, people from many other parts of the world were praying for him too.

We sent the results of the biopsy to our friends who were in

Oxford. They took it to the Radcliff hospital that specialised in cancer research. The report came back 'NO HOPE!' By then we had a great sense of peace, leaving him in the hands of God. As more and more time went by, and he was so well, even the doctors were amazed and said, 'If it doesn't recur within five years perhaps there could be hope.'

Jonnie continued to flourish and get into all kinds of mischief! When he was four he used to enjoy being taken for a ride on the farm tractor. One day, when I was busy serving the puddings at one of the conferences, he came bouncing in with, 'Mummy, I've been driving the tractor'. 'Have you darling.' I said absent-mindedly, continuing to serve. Suddenly a very white-faced tractor driver appeared and blurted out what had happened. Apparently, because the tractor was difficult to start, he had parked it on the side of a slope with its brakes on. As he was walking away he happened to glance back and to his horror saw the tractor rolling down the slope towards the river, a very happy four-year-old at the helm. Jonnie had successfully let off the brakes! Fortunately a pile of logs had saved him from plunging over the big drop into the river. Our children's guardian angel must have been working overtime! Now Jonnie is a strapping six-footer with a lovely Chilean wife, Prissie, and three children. For this we can only be eternally grateful to our Lord.

We were not the only members of our team to go through such parental anguish. Two of our new colleagues, Tom and Rene Curtis, who were living in Quepe, also suffered. Their little son, Tim, was Jonnie's friend, being about the same age. They often played together in the garden, mending the paths etc. One day Tim completely vanished, as if into thin air, so everyone was out looking for him. After a period of fruitless searching things began to look quite serious. Tony suddenly had an awful foreboding as the thought crossed his mind; could he possibly have fallen into the canal that flowed from the turbine in our mill? It seemed too dreadful to contemplate but, steeling himself, he went up to check.

Then he spotted a child's rubber ball floating down on the water. With an awful sinking feeling in the pit of his stomach, he realised that this meant that Tim must have fallen in and been swept away down stream. With a heavy heart he was about to raise the alarm and call all the searchers to switch their attention to the banks of the canal. Then came a shout of triumph from the farm; Tim had been found hiding under a bed in the house. His father had been cross with him over some minor misdemeanour and he had retreated there to avoid punishment. This little Tim is now working in the Paraguayan Chaco doing a glorious work among the indigenous people there.

In this case the anguish was short lived, and soon turned to joy. Sadly Tom and Rene passed through another agony that did not. Rene had just given birth to the sweetest baby girl. Then one morning, our nurse from Quepe hospital, Shirley Goodwin, sent over to the farm to ask if Tony and I could take her to the hospital in Temuco as she was anxious about the baby's condition. The hospital had been advised in advance to have an incubator ready. On arrival, I saw her into the incubator. The next morning I returned to the hospital and she seemed to be holding her own, this in spite of the fact that she was a blue baby and had a serious heart problem. Sadly the next day I received a phone call to say that she had died. Poor Rene was heart broken.

As I had never experienced this kind of thing before, I sought the help of our odd-job man. He went off and returned with a tiny white coffin. Back in the hospital a real shock awaited me. Clutching a permit to remove her little body, I was directed to the morgue. This was down a flight of steps and into a cold, damp, eerie basement. Dead bodies were lying all over the cement floor; each was covered with a sheet and had their name and number tied to a toe.

I gathered her up in a shawl and returning to the centre where I dressed her and laid her gently inside the coffin along with a rose I had picked from the garden. She looked so beautiful and peaceful just as if she were asleep. I was so relieved I had done this as Rene asked to see her; I only hoped it would help to ease some of her grief.

CHAPTER TWENTY-TWO

The 1960 earthquake

AT ABOUT 5 a.m. on Saturday, the 21st May 1960, we had a bad earthquake. Our three little girls rushed out of their bedroom and piled into our bed.

Later that same morning, while Tony was giving his lecture in the Institute, the second huge quake hit us. Suddenly his class was above him and then below him as the building heaved up and down. The extent of this movement in a wooden building is unbelievable. Of course, it was precisely because our houses had been constructed of wood, and were slightly raised off the ground on blocks, that they were able to absorb the shock; wood was the best material because it flexed under the strain, while the firmer windows popped out.

On that fateful night, Rosemary asked if she could sleep with Angelina Mena, our in-house Institute student, as she was so nervous after the two big shakes we had already had. Sure enough, a third massive quake struck us that night. Prompted by Angelina, they both stood together under the archway of the door until the worst of the movement had subsided; this was the safest place they could have chosen. The next morning we heard on the radio that the epicentre had been in the Concepción area and lots of houses had been brought down and many people killed.

All was relatively quiet for the Sunday morning service. This was memorable because we read Psalm 46, 'God is our refuge and strength, an ever present help in trouble. Therefore we will not fear, though the earth give way and the mountains fall into the heart of the sea, though its waters roar and foam and the mountains quake with their surging.' Surely God was preparing us for the ordeal that was to come.

At 3 p.m. on the Sunday afternoon we had the VERY big tremor. At precisely that time, the poor people in Concepción were burying their dead from the previous day's quakes. All our children, except for baby Jonnie, were in Sunday school over in the church. So Tony rushed upstairs to get him from his room while Angelina and I ran out of the house and took refuge in the middle of the field outside our garden gate. From there I watched, mesmerised, as our brick chimney swayed back and forth like a drunken man and then crashed to the ground; the wooden farmhouse itself looked just like a Walt Disney cartoon as it bulged in and out with every shock.

Meanwhile, Tony was wrestling to get into Jonnie's room because the bed had slidden across and jammed the door closed. Gradually he was able to ease the bed away sufficiently to get in and, snatching up Jonnie in his arms, he carried him down to us. Surprisingly, our only injury in all this was a minor bruise where Jonnie's little finger had been slightly crushed.

All this time the church bell kept ringing. I was so confused that I thought, 'What are they ringing the church bell for?' Then it dawned on me that it was the violence of the quake that was making it ring. An elderly man was caught in the middle of the suspension bridge when the quake struck. He clung on to the railing for dear life while the whole bridge whipped up and down, threatening to throw him off. Mercifully he survived.

Meanwhile, Tony was hastening up to the school to look for Bernardo who had been left there on his own. He found him lying in his cart, right under a high wall where he had been left in the shade. The wall was in danger of collapsing on him; if this had happened he would almost certainly have been crushed to death. But he was quietly praying and reading his New Testament that he had clasped between his shrivelled little hands. Tony grabbed the handles of the cart and made for the centre of the football pitch; this was the safest place to be. As they set off, the tremors intensified again, making the tops of the trees crash together above their heads. The ground itself was heaving like the waves of the sea; one moment he was shoving up hill, the next racing down the other side. At last they reached the relative safety of the pitch.

With Bernardo safe, Tony raced down the hill and across the suspension bridge to the church on the other side of the river where the children had been attending Sunday School with Shirley Goodwin, a nurse who had recently joined our team. To his great relief he found them all safe and sound in the orchard where they were quietly singing choruses to keep up their spirits. Shirley then told him of their narrow escape. To get out of the church, they had had to pass under the tower where the heavy bell was tolling. A moment after they were out, the bell had fallen on the very place where they had just been.

Next morning, the Monday, Tony drove to Temuco to get Terry who was in boarding school there. On the way, he found the concrete surface of the new paved highway all twisted and broken up. For his part, Terry was safe but he reported how many of his friends in Temuco who had claimed to be agnostic or atheist were, during the worst of the quakes, on their knees pleading for mercy from a God that they hadn't believed existed only a few moments before!

As far as we could tell, everyone was now safe, so Tony began to inspect the material damage back in Quepe. He already knew that the water tower had collapsed as we had seen the water from it streaming down the road. On going up to look, he found that it was now a mangled wreck. All our brick chimneys were down, our sewage system was smashed, the carpentry shop was ruined having slid about a hundred metres down the slope, the cement tube that had carried the water from the turbine was fragmented, the church bell was down and the dyke was badly cracked and leaking.

For my part, I had to make arrangements for the Institute

students' accommodation while the emergency lasted. For this, Shirley kindly offered to let them camp out on the veranda of the hospital. While the ominous rumblings continued, we opted to go outside where we slept on top of the lorry that was parked under the roof of an open barn. Here the floor was on a slight slope, so with each serious tremor the lorry, with its brakes off, would obligingly roll out into the open, clear of a possible collapsing roof; when things were calm, it remained under shelter. This really was a blessing as the weather began to turn nasty and we then had to contend with heavy drizzle on top of everything else. There we remained for about a week where I had to prepare our food on an open fire in the farmyard. Things were not made any easier for me when the cook decided to go home, leaving me with the task of providing meals for all the agricultural students as well as for our own family.

On Tuesday the 24th Tony began working on the dyke. He found that the damage was even worse than had been thought. There was an enormous amount of heavy debris to be removed. While he was still on this, Doug Milmine turned up with very bad news: the coastal towns of Toltén, Puerto Saavedra and Nehuentue had been totally flooded by a vast tidal wave, caused by the submarine quake. In view of this the two of them set off immediately to discover what had happened to Reg Bartle and Struggles who had been working there.

However, in Temuco they were greeted with the joyous news that they had escaped and had just arrived in town. Apparently a small boy had raised the alarm by shouted out, 'a huge mountain's coming in from the sea'. On hearing this, Reg climbed a tall tree; when he saw the size of the approaching wave he immediately urged everyone to flee to the top of a nearby hill. This was just as well as from there they watched with horror as the water rushed in and carried away many houses. Thanks to Reg's prompt action, the only person drowned was someone who returned from the hill to retrieve something from the house. Once the water had subsided sufficiently they went down only to find that the church roof had been destroyed and that the building itself had been lifted from its foundations of cement blocks and deposited some distance away. The sandbank that had previously protected the estuary of the river had completely disappeared, having sunk into the bed of the sea. Tony and Doug returned late that night to Quepe.

As Wednesday dawned, the radio reports became worse and worse. For our part, Tony and his helpers began to clear up the broken debris remaining from the fallen water tower and turbine. For this he used the winch of the Unimog. As he crept along the edge of the canal to get to the seat of action, the side suddenly gave way and one of the wheels went over. Only the great power of the Unimog allowed him to reverse out, without going over the edge, when the vehicle would have come down on top of him.

On Thursday the news was so bad of landslides and disasters in the hills that he decided he would volunteer to help with the Unimog. However, his offer was gratefully turned down, as by now the authorities had all the equipment they needed. So instead he took a friend, Bill Strong, to his centre in Pitrufquén, with food for the victims from Toltén. Here they were told of another miraculous escape. The ground had opened up and huge amounts of water had started gushing out of the splits. The people were only just able to scramble on to the roofs of the houses before the advancing surge swamped them. Others managed to get to higher ground and up trees, some even on the roof of the hotel. In this way they had escaped drowning.

Listening to the BBC we heard them announce that this was the most severe earthquake, in violence and in the extent of the area affected, since records started – but mercifully, not in actual deaths. The reason for our relatively low death rate was that the worst shock came on a Sunday, on a lovely sunny afternoon; consequently most families were out walking or playing in the parks or plazas, well out of reach of falling masonry. Later a report that all our people were safe was published on the front page of the Daily Telegraph. We certainly had much to be thankful for.

Over the next few days and weeks our team worked hard to cope with the aftermath of the disaster. They succeeded in getting the bell back into the tower. Tony began to put his library books back on their shelves! One of our people had been separated from his family in the quake. They tracked down both him and his separated family and managed to reunite them by lending them an empty house in Chol Chol.

We also sent a team of young people in the Unimog to do the immediate repairs on our church in the coastal town of Nehuentue. Later, another team, including Terry, went to finish the job and combine it with a series of special meetings in the church. At the end of a strenuous day they were all looking forward hungrily to the meal Struggles had prepared for them. After this they planned to have a short service of thanksgiving in the church at which Terry had been asked to speak.

Now Struggles was undoubtedly one of the world's best women; but she was also one of the world's worst cooks! During her visits to rural areas in her caravan, she would go blackberrying. With the fruit, she made jam for herself and others and, for economy, she would store this in rusty old tins. The jam was usually delicious but a bit hazardous; occasionally an unopened tin would explode, blowing off the lid and making an incredible mess. Doug Milmine, although a great fan of Struggles, was scathing about her cooking. He used to call her tins of jam 'Purple Peril' and one of her favourite dishes she served, 'Tramp's neck stew'. This meal for the lads was no exception! The single dish on the menu was another of her favourite recipes – a rich, fish soup. On other occasions when Terry had been given this, he could at least find plenty of clear soup, once he had broken a thin crust of fat on the surface.

On this occasion, determined to do her very best for her hungry young helpers, there was so much crust of fat that there was hardly any room left for the liquid soup beneath. Then, horror of horrors, floating in the soup, Terry began to find eyeballs from the fish. These, Struggles explained, were to add further body to the soup, in order to satisfy their appetites. This was just too much for Terry. In the middle of the night he just couldn't keep his meal down any longer. Racing out of the church where they were all sleeping, he was violently sick. When dear Struggles heard what had happened, she was most concerned. 'The poor lad' she sympathised, 'It must have been because he was so nervous after preaching in church'!

We now began receiving reports of an ugly resurgence of pagan Mapuche superstitions. Some of these rituals were being held at one of their sacred places called the 'Monopaine' on the road from Quepe to Temuco. Apparently a young girl had started prophesying and this was being accompanied by sinister outbursts against foreigners, both English and Chileans alike; we were being blamed for bringing down the wrath of the spirits and thus causing the earthquake. There were strange dances and painting of the face and one or two of our people had been going to these. One Machi on the coast had even resorted to human sacrifice, offering up a little child, in an attempt to propitiate the angry spirits of the sea.

Undeterred, we continued to do all we could to alleviate the suffering of those affected in our area. For this, we were so grateful for a massive influx of aid from the United States that we were able to distribute to the most stricken families.

By an extraordinary coincidence, we also lived through the second largest earthquake that hit Chile. This was over twenty years later, when we were 'retired' in England. We were on one of our three return visits to help our SEAN team in the delightful coastal town of Viña del Mar. Although by grades on the Richter scale this earthquake was slightly less in intensity than the one in 1960, in an urban setting with its brick and concrete buildings, we personally were more affected than when among the wooden buildings in the South.

One day in March, 1985, Tony and I were alone in the large SEAN centre. This was situated under a towering cliff. On the top of this were a lookout platform and a number of large trees. The force of the quake cracked the walls and filled the building with dense dust clouds and fine debris. As we embraced each other in the doorway of our room we really did think that we were going to die and just committed ourselves to the Lord. The concrete look-out balcony came down and missed our building by a fraction on one side and shortly after one of the huge trees above fell down the cliff and smashed its way down the alley outside our kitchen window, cutting off all the outside light. Thus we were spared to live on to finish our work on the SEAN courses for some sixteen more years; and of course to write this book.

CHAPTER TWENTY-THREE

Family antics in Temuco

EARLY IN 1961 we moved into Temuco to replace the Milmines who were starting our new centre in the capital, Santiago. Tony, however, continued to go out daily to lecture in the Quepe Institute. For the first time in years all our family were under one roof; except for Hilary, that is. She so loved the quiet country life and people in Quepe that she asked if she could stay there with Shirley. As Shirley liked Hilary as much as the other way round, this was agreed.

As usual, it didn't take our kids long before they began to stamp their mark on the place! For example, thrilled by the nice wide pavements in Temuco, Rosemary decided to get some much-needed practice on her skates. Gathering speed, she went careering down the street, narrowly missing a number of outraged pedestrians. The problem was that she had not yet mastered the art of stopping. On this occasion, this problem was solved abruptly when she crashed into a street vendor's cider barrel. Desperately she grabbed at the first thing that came to hand which happened to be the tap of the barrel. Out came the bung and so did all the cider, as it gurgled away down the gutter. Before the poor man could gather his wits, Rosemary had slipped off her skates and done a bunk. Terrified that the police might be in hot pursuit and that she would be put in prison, she tore back into the house and locked herself securely in the loo. This, of course, was a great embarrassment to us, especially as we only heard about it later and couldn't make amends for the poor man's losses.

But it wasn't all one-sided. Two of our young lady colleagues also had a brush with a street vendor; this one was selling cooking oil. He came banging urgently on the door to say that his tin drum had sprung a leak and his oil was oozing away. If the Señoritas could lend him a really big saucepan he might be able to save some and would then give them a little for their kindness. The girls rushed into the kitchen and got the biggest saucepan they could find and off went the vendor to save what oil he could. The girls waited patiently for his return! This time it was the vendor that came out on top because, of course, the girls never did see the saucepan again!

Our seven-year-old Pattie also had her scrapes. She was having an unhappy patch at school. However, she had gone off happily enough each morning in her uniform, was back for lunch at the usual time and then off again for afternoon classes, so I didn't suspect anything. I only discovered that she had been playing truant when I got a call from the headmistress to ask whether Pattie was ill, as she hadn't been to school for a week.

When I tackled her, it turned out that she had spent every day in the home of some friends she had made nearby.

Tony was very upset about this but I have to admit that I had a head start over him when it came to understanding what it was that made our Pattie tick on these occasions. For example, when I was also seven and living in Southport, Mummy had to join Daddy in London to look for another home. We were staying temporarily in lodgings not far away from my school. As Mummy had to catch the 8 o'clock coach for London the next morning, she reluctantly had to leave me in the school as a boarder.

I hated this. So when I went to bed that night I thought, 'If I don't get back to Mummy now, it will be too late'. While everyone was asleep, I crept out of bed in my pyjamas, put my Teddy and a few treasures into my tiny suitcase, and made my way down the stairs and into the dining room. There I managed to push up the sash window, threw my suitcase out and followed it. By a miracle I cleared the invisible basement by inches.

I picked up my suitcase, and under the hissing gas lamps, with moths flying round them, I ran all along the railings of the park back to Mummy's digs. The landlady, with rag curlers in her hair, came to the door in her night-clothes. Horrified, she went immediately to get Mummy who popped me into her bed while she got dressed and then went straight round to the school. They were not at all pleased and didn't want me back; Mummy didn't want me to stay anyway. She packed up my things and we still managed to catch the 8 o'clock coach to London where Daddy met us. After this, Pattie's truancy didn't seem quite so bad.

Jonnie was only two and a half at the time so you wouldn't have thought that he could have done much to make his mark on the town. However he did! He used to rock his cot so that it walked across his small bedroom until it was under the window from which he could get a good view of all that was going on below.

Although there was a bar across the window, I didn't put it

past him to climb through it. I therefore had a screw put in a floorboard well away from the window and the leg of the cot anchored to it. A few days later, there was a ring at the door and when I opened it to a stranger she asked, 'Do you know that there is a little child up on the second floor standing on the windowsill?' I tore upstairs and this time I found that he had turned his chamber pot upside down and by balancing on top of it on tiptoe had just managed to climb up on to the sill.

I also managed to get myself into an awkward predicament when I was in the Temuco centre. I enjoyed taking part in our lively Dorcas meetings, just as I had done when I was in Chol Chol. On one rather memorable occasion we were all sitting in our large ground floor sitting room making simple garments for needy children. I noticed that a lorry had drawn up outside the window. Inside the cabin I could see a frightened young mother clutching her baby. Out got an obviously furious driver hauling a terrified little boy of about three by his hair. Then he began undoing his belt buckle ready to thrash him. I couldn't believe my eyes and on impulse leapt up, threw open the window and jumping out ordered him to stop.

Although obviously taken aback he told me to mind my own business. So I called through the window to the others to phone the police. At that moment a formidable figure sailed into view round the corner like a battleship with all its guns blazing. It was our neighbour, the German wife of the garage owner from the opposite side of our street. This Frau was famous for striking terror into the tough male work force in the garage. We always knew when she had come on the scene because the hammering which was slowing down suddenly burst into action again. I thankfully left her to it and crept back into the house with my heart thumping fit to burst.

I seemed to make a speciality of getting to know strong women from among the ethnic communities. I used to visit an elderly anglo-chilean lady called Annie Smith who was bed-ridden. I really enjoyed her stories of past days in Temuco. She would leave her front door unlocked so that her friends could come in and out without bothering her, so I didn't have to get her to answer the door each time I visited her. A little concerned about this on security grounds I said to her, 'Aren't you afraid, Annie, to live here all alone, with the front door on the latch?' She didn't say a word but just turned back the corner of her pillow and lovingly patted a loaded revolver that was lying there. Henceforth we always referred to her among ourselves as 'Pistol-packing Annie'.

But to return to Jonnie's antics! Even at that early age, he was a real mimic. For example, he could imitate the call of the newspaper boys to perfection with their distinctive high-pitched cry of 'Diario, diario' (Papers, papers). This was something of an embarrassment when I took him down town with me and he would suddenly come out with this call. To my chagrin I would see people everywhere looking around perplexed to discover where on earth the newspaper boy was.

From his little corner bedroom Jonnie could hear the fire-engines roar by at full speed. Their distinctive warning sirens could be heard for miles; 'Pa poo, pa poo, pa poo'. So whenever we passed his room we would hear a perfect imitation coming out from Jonnie: 'Pa poo, pa poo, pa poo'. These fire-engines were in constant demand in Temuco. Most of the buildings were constructed of wood; this was the cheapest material as it came in abundance from the enormous forests to the south. As we've seen, it was also the most appropriate material because it was more likely to withstand the shock of a major earthquake. But there was a down side – the danger of fire.

The first fire we saw there occurred at 2 a.m. in the morning when we were awakened by the sirens of the fire-engines. From the top of our house we could see everything that went on. The flames were leaping at least a hundred feet into the air. In the morning we went to see the burnt-out site; only a shell was left, but the wooden houses on either side were completely untouched. However, the tragic price paid was two firemen who perished in the blaze.

It is easy to understand, therefore, why the International Fire Brigades in Temuco were so respected. They were all volunteers. Each ethnic community, such as the Italians and Germans, had their own distinctive colour of uniform and they looked very smart. They were, of course, immensely proud of their own unit. Because many people owed their property, if not their lives, to the bravery of these men, they were immensely popular. If one of them got killed in the course of duty, the whole town would turn out at the funeral. These were always held at night so that the processions, lit up by flaming torches and led by their own band playing one of the funeral marches, were a most moving spectacle.

The efficient fire-engines in Temuco carried me back to our early days in Chol Chol where we had our fair share of house fires. We could certainly have done with one of the Temuco fire-engines in those days but unfortunately the long distance and dreadful state of the roads made it impossible for them to reach us in time. So we were thrown on to our very meagre local resources.

I vividly remember one such occasion, when I had invited the Señoritas over to supper. I had asked Dominga, our resident Mapuche school girl, to make up the log fire. Coming from the country, she was more used to an open campfire. So she took me literally and piled the logs right up the chimney, which then caught fire. The next thing we heard was the church bell tolling; this was the recognised alarm for alerting the village when there was a fire.

I came running down the stairs to be met by half the village pouring into the house: children, dogs, adults armed with buckets of water. It was pandemonium. Without asking me, they started passing out all the furniture through the windows. They hurled buckets of water in the vague direction of the chimney where most of it bounced back into the room and gushed all over the floor. All I could do was stand helplessly by and plan how I was

167

going to clear up the mess once they had gone.

At supper, Miss Royce admonished me, 'Really, my dear! You must keep your chimneys clean'. A month later we heard the church bell tolling again. This time it was the hospital that was on fire. We all dashed over to help. They had an added problem; one of the nurses told us that a number of drums of highly flammable paraffin were stored all round the balcony. By now the fire had begun to get into the wooden tiles just above these drums. So Tony had to climb up in an attempt to remove the burning tiles before they could cause a major explosion and even burn down the hospital. It was hairy stuff, especially as he had not been trained as a fireman! Mercifully this fire, too, was eventually brought under control. All this time poor Miss Royce was quietly weeping, for fear of losing her beloved hospital. I just couldn't bring myself to say, 'Miss Royce, you really must keep your chimneys clean!'

In Chol Chol, we did have a fire-brigade of sorts. They were a group of chaps that did a reasonably good job by passing buckets of water down the line; something like I have just described. On visits to Temuco, they had seen some of the fire-brigades there. Inspired by their smart uniforms, they felt they needed to get their own act together. So one day a delegation arrived on our doorstep asking for a donation towards obtaining a fire-engine and uniforms. They could make the fire-engine out of a large water drum, mounted on wheels, plus a good pump. Would we give a donation? For such a good cause, how could we say no?

Time passed, and we heard nothing. On enquiring, we were told that their collection had been a great success. The only problem was that it was not enough to buy both the fire-engine and the uniforms. Their board had given this careful consideration. Because you couldn't have a real fire-brigade without proper uniforms, they had finally voted to buy these. And guess what! A short time later their fire station burnt down!

CHAPTER TWENTY-FOUR

Farewell Chile!

OUR MOVE into Temuco, where we spent our last two years in Chile, was all part of a new and ambitious plan to break out of our rather limited patch in Mapuche territory by entering some of the major Chilean cities. Our hope was that eventually we would have an Anglican Diocese for Chile, with Doug Milmine as its first bishop. This we felt would reflect more accurately the unique and colourful culture of this Republic. From our earliest days our ultimate goal had been to achieve the transition from foreign mission to national church with its own Chilean pastors and bishops. Doug's move to the capital, Santiago, was all part of this plan.

The English-speaking bishop at that time was based in Buenos Aires in Argentina. Although his jurisdiction was over a number of South American Republics, originally this mainly entailed the oversight of a limited number of British chaplaincy churches and the indigenous work of SAMS; for this responsibility he had not needed Spanish. But now that the work was growing so quickly in this language his ministry was becoming increasingly untenable. This was another reason for our desire to see each Republic eventually with its own diocese and Episcopal oversight in the language of the people.

Our hopes were fuelled by a steady flow of new colleagues all with a mandate to work in Spanish. A number of these had resulted from our contacts when on our first home leave in the UK and Tony's visit to Australia on his way back. For example I have already explained how Kath Clark and Aphra Ward were now both working in our Quepe Training Institute; these were just two of such contacts.

Others of our new colleagues began to move into some of the larger cities. One couple, Leo and Pat Hunter, settled into Concepción, on the Pacific coast; this was the former home of Ian Morrison. We also began to think of entering another city on the Pacific Coast, Valparaiso (known as 'Valpo' among the British Community). This was the large port to the north-west of Santiago; we had embarked from here on the 'Reina del Mar' on our way back for our first home leave five years ago.

In the heyday of British commercial expansion in Chile, a large ex-patriot community had grown up on 'Cerro Alegre' (Happy Hill) high above the port of Valpo. Commensurate with this they had built a vast Anglican Church that in those days was well-filled with an English-speaking congregation. It was also graced with one of the finest pipe-organs in South America. It now lay empty and abandoned. As the local population had gradually changed to Spanish-speaking, it was our hope to establish a new congregation there in that language. Our kind hostess, Mrs. Hemans, who had seen us off on the 'Reina', had a son called Michael. He was a distinguished organist, well known for his recitals in London. Michael now offered to play the organ if we recommenced services there.

When in Theological College, Tony had become a firm friend of David Pytches. We had met up with him again more recently in the UK when we were at a House Party in Oxford. He, and his wife Mary, had now joined us. This young couple was not only willing to take on any challenge but David was also a skilled handyman. He offered to build a living apartment at one end of the huge church hall in Valpo, where they could eventually settle down comfortably. It doesn't take a lot of imagination to realise that they were far from comfortable during the prolonged period of construction.

Once this was accomplished, David began to build a second apartment at the other end of the hall to accommodate another couple. In Australia, Tony had formed another close friendship with two students in Sydney. They were now married and we were thrilled when Greg and Judy Blaxland joined us in Temuco. Once they had polished up their Spanish and got accustomed to the new culture they moved into the other apartment in Valpo. The Pytches and Blaxlands did a great work together in building up a new Spanish-speaking congregation.

Just before we left Chile we had another influx of new colleagues. This time there were three new couples and a single nurse. It fell to my lot to receive them in Temuco and make them as comfortable as possible. I got off to a rather shaky start. We had just built a 'Caupolicán Wing' on to the small Temuco house. It had a neat row of three visitors' bedrooms that led off from a corridor with the large boys' dormitory at the end. I threw open the three doors and began allocating a room to each couple. As I did so, I detected a startled expression flit across the face of one of the wives. Confusing their names, I had ushered her into a bedroom with someone else's husband! Fortunately they were a long-suffering bunch and with their kind help I managed to untangle the muddle!

One of these three couples was Brian and Gill Skinner. As you may recall, our friendship with Brian dated back to our Slough days but this was the first time that I had met Gill. Brian had been one of the smartest lads in our Boys Brigade Bugle Band when Tony was the Chaplain there. He had since graduated from an agricultural college and had now come out to run the Quepe farm.

Before we left Chile, Colin and Barbara Bazley also joined our team. David, Colin and Brian all later became bishops in Chile. These Spanish-speaking missionaries were an important start to our ultimate goal of achieving a truly national church. Even more important was to give official recognition to the gifts of leadership among our Chilean brethren. In our Anglican Church this was by ordination. The English-speaking fraternity had long opposed our requests for this; now at last the bishop had agreed and we were presenting four excellent candidates. One of these was Ian Morrison, grandson of Daddy Wilson, the bank clerk we had first met in Concepción.

For this important event all our Chile staff congregated in Temuco; so did many of our members from the Quepe and Chol Chol districts. A group had even come down from the Chaplaincy church in Santiago, Douglas having persuaded them to take part – in itself a mini-miracle. Everything had been carefully planned; I had the heavy responsibility of providing refreshments for the widely differing tastes of the leaders of each visiting ethnic group. There was an air of suppressed excitement and a happy buzz of conversation as friends long-absent from each other began catching up on all their news.

Tony and the other pastors had organised the ordination ceremony itself. The church was packed with over four hundred present. It looked resplendent in its new coat of paint inside and out which we had just finished in time for the great event. Also the newly installed lighting transformed and brightened the whole service.

Over the last two years an excellent choir had developed in Temuco. We actually won the competition for best church choir that year. Their beautiful anthem further enhanced this solemn occasion. The bishop, not easily impressed with our simple Spanish services, was really moved and appreciative. He turned to Tony and said, 'This must have been a very great day for you and your colleagues'.

Tony was happy that the English-speaking group seemed to have fitted in so well. He had done everything he could to make the service acceptable to them. So it was a bit of a shock when chatting to one of them afterwards the following exchange took place. To Tony's 'Oh! Wasn't it a wonderful united service?' he received the reply, 'No! I'm afraid I can't agree'. 'But what could you possibly have taken exception too?' Tony enquired. 'Well', came the extraordinary answer, 'Didn't you see the shoes of your fellow who helped the bishop administer the Holy Communion?

They were brown under his black cassock'. 'Well!' Tony replied, barely containing himself, 'Frankly you were lucky he had shoes on at all. Many of our Indian leaders are great men of God but some would have been barefooted. I'm sure God doesn't mind'.

Years later, after our Hilary had married Alf Cooper and we were visiting them in their church in Santiago, to his horror Tony spotted this same fellow bearing down on him. Unable to make his escape, he found himself enveloped in a bear-like hug. 'You must have thought I was an absolute cad when I criticised your priest in Temuco' he said. 'You'll be glad to know that since then I've become a real Christian under Alf's ministry. Please forgive me'. Of course, rejoicing, Tony did just that.

But to return to the service of ordination! Throughout his stay, the bishop had become increasingly unwell and had developed a high temperature. However, determined not to disappoint us, he insisted on carrying on with the service. But strangely he had asked Doug Milmine if he would travel back to Santiago with him on the evening coach the very night of the ordination. As the time approached, I felt sure that he should cancel this arrangement and stay an extra day or two in bed at our home to give himself time to recover. Accordingly, I went to his room and pleaded with him to do this. His extraordinary response was 'My Dear! I have to go tonight, even if they carry me there in my coffin'. He was always very sweet with our children and took a special liking to Rosemary. She was also in bed with what turned out to be appendicitis and so before leaving he popped his head around the door and said, 'Goodbye, Darling. Remember, no flowers'. These were his last words to her before setting off on what turned out to be his last journey. He seemed to have had the strangest premonition.

Early next morning at 6 a.m. we received a phone call from Doug breaking the shocking news that the bishop was dead and that Doug was in custody in the police station in San Carlos. According to a rather strange Chilean law, the one accompanying a deceased person had to be put in prison until it was proved that they were not responsible for the death. Doug had volunteered to be that person rather than the bus driver. Greg Blaxland was still staying with us in Temuco at the time and he immediately offered to accompany Tony on his journey to help Doug out of his predicament and to do all that was necessary to prepare the bishop's body for burial. They also had to purchase a coffin, arrange for the post-mortem and obtain a burial pass to authorise them to take the body to Santiago.

They set off together in the long-bodied Land Rover that would allow them to transport the coffin north. On arrival in San Carlos they made their way immediately to the tribunal to see how Douglas was faring. He told us the dreadful details of the bishop's end. Still feeling extremely unwell, he had asked for the bus to stop. Dazzled by the headlights of a second bus that had pulled up behind, the bishop had mistaken the parapet of a bridge for the curb and in stepping forward had disappeared into the deep gully, striking his head violently on the concrete edge as he fell. When Doug and the drivers had succeeded in pulling him up it was plain that he couldn't possibly survive. One of the buses drove the bishop at speed to the nearest hospital in Parral twenty minutes away but he had died on the way.

Leaving Doug to give his details to the officials in San Carlos, they then set off in an attempt to get the necessary documents for removing the body. Here they encountered a frustrating situation – the bishop's accident had occurred in San Carlos in one province but he had died in Parral in a neighbouring one; neither province wanted to take responsibility! After ceaseless shuttling between the two, at last San Carlos sent a telegram to grant permission for the authorities in Parral to issue them with the documents.

Meanwhile Douglas had been released and so all three of them spent the night in an inadequate hotel in Parral where they constantly had to shift their beds around to avoid the rain which streamed in through the leaky roof. The following morning they went to the morgue where they found the poor bishop lying on the floor where he had been thrown. They did all they could to make him look presentable especially by shaving him and cleaning up his face. With Greg's strength they then laid him gently in his coffin. It took all the rest of the morning to get the certificate from the doctor, having eventually to track him down in his own house. Over the phone they had been told that the British ambassador in Santiago had arranged for the funeral service to start at 7 p.m. By the time they left they knew that they couldn't possibly make it before 7.30.

However, the moment everything was in order they set off at high speed on the 350 kilometres remaining to reach Santiago. Bedraggled and exhausted they reached the church at exactly 7.30 p.m. only to find the congregation singing the final hymn. They were told that the ambassador had to attend a cocktail party at 7.15 p.m. and so it was impossible for them to wait.

With all these ups-and-downs we had certainly come a long way from the time when Tony was the only ordained missionary working in Spanish in Chile. We now had a much increased and very capable missionary staff and the first nationals had been ordained. Even the sad death of the bishop meant that the Anglican authorities were now considering what we had for so long desired, a diocese in Chile with our own Spanish-speaking bishop, hopefully Doug Milmine. So we felt we could move on with the satisfaction of knowing that the work would be left in Doug's most capable hands. Early the next year, 1963, we were bidding all our friends in Chile a last and emotional farewell before we were off to England for our second home leave, this time to return, not to Chile, but to Paraguay.

When we were in England again, Tony had a strange experience on his way to a meeting in Westminster. Along with the bustling crowd he was rushing down Parliament Square when the lights changed to red and everyone piled up on the edge of the curb. At green, they all set off again, jostling each other as they went. Suddenly, Tony's heart missed a beat; he was walking shoulder to shoulder with the person he had last seen when he had laid him to rest in his coffin in Chile – it was none other than Bishop Evans! At this extraordinary apparition, Tony began pinching himself to find out if he was really awake. He was then just about to pinch the other fellow to find out if he was a ghost when suddenly he recalled hearing that Bishop Evans had had an identical twin. So instead, he turned to the chap and asked, 'Excuse me, are you Bishop Evan's brother?' Taken aback by this unusual enquiry from a complete stranger and in the middle of a zebra crossing in Parliament Square, the reply came somewhat brusquely, 'Yes! But who the devil are you?' He was staggered to learn that Tony had been in Chile on that fateful day and had actually helped to care for his brother's dead body on that stretch of desolate road midway between Temuco and Santiago.

CHAPTER TWENTY-FIVE

The two Paraguays

THE TIME had come for us to return to South America but now not to Chile but to Paraguay. Suddenly we woke up to the fact that because we were going by sea we would arrive too late to enrol the children in their new schools or, in Terry's case, the University. This was very important if they were to avoid missing a whole academic year, so Terry kindly volunteered to go ahead by air to take care of these arrangements for us.

We went to Heathrow to see him off. There, we got talking with an English gentleman who had lived in Chile. As you will probably have gathered, we were not very popular with some of the English community there because they objected to us holding our services in Spanish. However, we began chatting with him pleasantly enough. Then suddenly he asked, 'By the way, where did you live in Chile?' 'In the South' we said, 'Mostly in Temuco and the surrounding parts'. 'My goodness' came back the reply, 'Did you by any chance bump into that terrible Canon Tony Barratt when you were there?' There was a moment of strained silence finally broken by Tony pronouncing, 'Yes! I am he'. The poor fellow literally staggered back with embarrassment, hitting his head against a pillar. 'Oh!' he gasped, 'I had imagined you to be some cantankerous old prelate!' 'Well! That's for you to decide now that you've met me' Tony responded.

Finally, we too were on our way. On the voyage out to Buenos Aires we already knew most of the ports of call because this was our second time on this Atlantic route. What was a totally new experience was the six-day trip up the River Paraná, from Buenos Aires to Asunción, the capital of Paraguay. The river steamer was very comfortable, our small cabin had windows looking directly on to the deck giving us a clear view of the exotic vegetation and wildlife as we glided by.

We were told that the Paraná is an exceptionally difficult river to navigate so it needed a highly skilled pilot who rarely leaves the bridge. At times the banks almost closed in on us on each side. At other times they were so far apart that we could hardly see them; it was just as if we were in open sea. As we passed the nearer banks, groups of alligators would slide silently off the sandbanks into the water and monkeys were chattering and playing in the palm trees. We even saw a toucan.

Although the heat was insufferable we got some relief when a tremendous storm broke over us. The lightening zipped and flashed up and down the metal railing around the deck and just yards away from the window of our cabin. This storm followed us right up to Asunción and so we arrived in torrential rain. There, Terry and a number of the Paraguayan team were waiting to meet us on the quay. On disembarking we drove to our centre through rivers of water that came shooting down the steep hill from each side street. The force of the water was so great that people were throwing their rubbish into the streets where it was swept away into the harbour! Later we learnt that these torrents could lift out the iron grids covering the drains. People had been known to disappear down one of these and were then swept along the underground drains into the river below and drowned.

At our new mission station we were welcomed warmly by the rest of the team. Our bungalow was lovely with cool, stone floors and wooden slatted shutters to catch every breath of fresh air – and my word did we need it! Our bath had been made of tiles and let into the floor like a miniature swimming pool. Once we had bid goodbye to our friends we all made a dive for it. We used to fill it with cold water each morning and then all of us would slide in and out whenever we had the least chance.

Paraguay was situated in the very heart of South America and therefore was completely land-locked. It was divided into two by the mighty River Paraguay, the continuation northwards of the Paraná up which we had just travelled. The two sides could hardly have been more different. To the east there was gently undulating terrain that was criss-crossed by roads that connected its big cities and towns. To the west lay the Chaco where as far as the eye could reach there was not a hill to be seen. Here there were no towns and only one road to serve the whole area. It was carved up into vast cattle ranches with their isolated homesteads. Each had its small airstrip.

On most ranches there was a group of Enthlit[1] people. No longer having land of their own, they had squatted there and were used as cheap labour by the wealthy ranch owners where they had become their virtual serfs. As the Enthlit had been denied Paraguayan citizenship they were considered to be little more than animals and therefore with no human rights in law.

As we became more familiar with each side of the river, we realised that here we were really dealing with two distinct Paraguays, not just one. As if to highlight this difference, sophisticated Asunción stood proudly on the east side of the river. Although small in comparison to most of the capital cities of the continent, for us it was by far the biggest South American town we had worked in. The President's palace was quite impressive albeit badly pockmarked by bullets and shells that had hit it during the numerous revolutions. Old-fashioned trams ran down the main streets; it also had a railway station, a large port, a high-rise hotel and wealthy suburbs with their luxury houses, mostly owned by relatives of the president or members of his government, army or police force. The inhabitants were nearly all bilingual, speaking Spanish and Guaraní; this was a result of the union of the early colonising Spanish men with the indigenous Guaraní women.

On the other side of the river and buried away in the Paraguayan Chaco was Makthlawaiya, a tract of land of about 7,000 acres. This was very small compared with the average

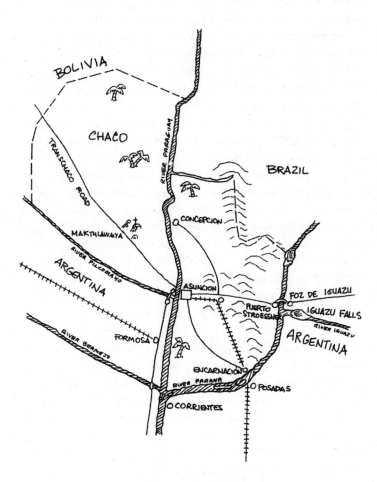

Paraguay in 1965

Chaco ranch. It belonged to our mission that had set up a small reservation for the Enthlit people there. Our missionaries had spent many faithful years helping and teaching them in their native language. But now these people were gradually picking up enough Guaraní from the ranch owners to be able to communicate in that language as well. Only a very small proportion of them, however, could speak Spanish.

The Enthlit people that had taken refuge in Makthlawaiya were better off than most of those on the ranches. Their children could attend our mission school, we had a nurse or nurses to provide them with basic medical care and they had been given plots of land to cultivate. They also had a large church building where they attended very lively services.

Our task was to find ways of linking these 'two Paraguays' to the advantage of both. Obviously a major link was the language of Guaraní that both the indigenous Chaco people and the Asunción city dwellers could speak.

Another wide gap between the two Paraguays was the physical one, as there were no roads by which to travel between Asunción and Makthlawaiya. We bridged this gap through the services of a friendly pilot in the 'Missionary Aviation Fellowship' who would fly us in at a reasonable price. As we in Asunción had twice-daily radio contact with our Chaco colleagues, we would then purchase all the provisions that they had ordered and send them up to them on the next plane.

But perhaps the most memorable and charming of our attempts to link Asunción and Makthlawaiya was when we brought down ten young Enthlit children from the primary school for a week's visit in the capital. It all started when a kind benefactor gave us a sum of money to do with it whatever we wanted. After much thought we decided to use it to finance this visit. So we asked the teachers to select the ten best pupils and hoped that this in itself would be an incentive to higher standards. So it proved to be. When all was ready we booked a trip there and back in the Cessna aeroplane; once the seats were removed there was room for them all to sit around on the floor. It was a very happy little band of children that alighted in the airport.

We prepared two dormitories, one for the girls and the other for the boys, and simple food, the type that they were used to and liked. Our difficulty was that we knew nothing of their language and they could hardly speak a word of Spanish. To us, their language sounded like an unintelligible stream of clicks and clacks with a frequent 'isssst', which seemed to be their way of expressing utter amazement.

First we introduced them to the novelty of the telephone, taking two groups into homes some distance apart. Their faces were a study as they heard their friends in their own language speaking to them down the line. They just couldn't make out how the device could know their Enthlit language nor how their friends could be heard when they knew that they were so far away. We then added treats to which they were unaccustomed. Their reaction to the cold of an ice-cream, which they had never tasted before, was highly entertaining. They dissolved into hilarious giggles with each lick.

In the city centre was a high-rise luxury hotel called the Hotel Guaraní. At that time it was the tallest building in Paraguay. For children that had only seen small wooden single-story huts or bungalows it must have seemed like fairyland. The lifts caused squeals of delight tinged with terror as they ascended and descended. The panoramic view from the top was awe-inspiring even for us. It left our kids from the Chaco completely stunned. They gazed in amazement at the mighty River Paraguay as it wound its way southward.

We then told them that we were going to take them on a boat on this very river. The captain was marvellously helpful when he realised where the children had come from. He took them on the bridge, showed them all the impressive instruments and explained their use in simple Guaraní. He then escorted them down to the engine room. We were so grateful for such co-

operation in our project.

From the riverboat we went to the railway station. Paraguay still sported a number of grand old steam trains that snorted their way along the lines. The engine driver, too, was super. He agreed to take the kids in his cabin, showed them how to feed the fires and how to blow the whistle. You can just imagine the reaction that this caused. Finally he kindly took them in small groups for a short run up the line and back. The children were ecstatic.

Asunción had only recently acquired a supermarket, so the day before they left I gave them each a little money to get presents to take back for their families. Rosemary and Hilary helped to organise them and so we set off gleefully to do this shopping. We were amazed at their restraint in their purchases; such useful things as pasta, sugar, maté (their national equivalent of our tea), lentils and the like. They all piled these into the single trolley so I began to wonder how they were going to remember what was theirs at the checkout. But without any fuss each one

184

picked out and put on the counter their own pile of purchases and paid accordingly. It caused quite a sensation among the staff. Each child then received an additional keepsake to add to his or her pile. All was gratefully received as they stored it away to share later with their families. We found the children's manners to be impeccable throughout.

We received exactly the same kind treatment when we went to the stationer's shop. They were given exercise books, rubbers, pencil sharpeners and coloured crayons. Once again, it was a very happy group of Enthlit children that returned to base that night. On the way back, as we passed a shop window, one of them stretched out his hand to touch something; he was completely mystified when it went smack into the glass, another thing they had never met before.

On the final day we took them to the shore of the nearby Lake Ipacaraí. As they passed each hill there were further gasps of astonishment; their land was as flat as a pancake. At the water's edge the boys flung off their clothes with abandon and plunged into the lake completely starkers, without so much as a blush. Here at least they were in their element and swam around in and under the water like a shoal of little fish. The girls were slightly more circumspect and shyly crept in with their panties on. When one of the boys came across a stone on the beach he was spellbound; but gradually this turned to excitement as he picked it up and began to play with it. Cautiously the others all followed suit. A little collection of stones now became one of their most treasured possessions – there are no stones in the Chaco!

It was an eye-opener to see how children that had never seen any of these things before reacted with such dignity to a totally new environment. It was one of the most rewarding experiences we had ever had. It would be hard to decide who enjoyed it the most – we adults, the children, or their astonished friends and families when on their return they poured out their story in an excited stream of clicks and clacks, liberally punctuated with many an 'isssst'.

After we had formed our family musical group, with Paraguayan harps and acoustic guitars, we were able to reverse the process. This time, we flew up to our friends in Makthlawaiya rather than the other way around. Sadly I was not able to go, as there would not have been room in the tiny Cessna plane. Only Terry, Rosemary, Hilary and Tony could fit in and even then they all had to lie on the floor with the instruments laid on top of them. But they certainly felt it was all worth while. A vast crowd of people came in from far and wide so that the large church was packed to the doors; there was still a huge over-flow outside that listened attentively through the windows as well. So in these simple ways we did our best to bridge the huge cultural divide between the 'Two Paraguays'.

1 Usually this is spelt 'Enxet' but as it is pronounced 'Enthlit' I have spelt it phonetically throughout.

CHAPTER TWENTY-SIX

The 'Humming Birds' are hatched

OUR FAMILY musical group had very much enjoyed visiting Makthlawaiya. It led to further engagements including one across the border in Argentina. As we had such a splendid and gifted mission team in Paraguay, Tony was able to leave most of the day-to-day running of the different departments to them. Increasingly his contribution was one of general oversight and visitation of his enormous area. Gradually he also got involved in the formation of this family musical group and its use.

Our initial involvement with the Paraguayan harp started by a chance encounter with one of the leading harpists in the land, Sr. Cortesi. Paraguay was a country with a very small population, there were only about 400,000 inhabitants in the capital city of Asunción. Whereas in a larger city it would have been unlikely for us to get an introduction to the top musicians, Paraguay was such a small country that this was possible.

It so happened that at that time Sr. Cortesi was teaching the harp to one of Rosemary's close school friends, Dolly Sosa! On one occasion, when Dolly was having her harp lesson, Rosemary had popped in to visit her. Never slow to get on to a good thing, Rosemary cheekily asked if she could have a go. Sr. Cortesi was so impressed with her flair for the instrument that later he kindly offered to give her and Hilary joint lessons for the price of one.

At the time, Terry had been learning to play the classical guitar from another top Paraguayan musician, so gradually we began to conceive the idea of forming a harp trio by getting Terry to accompany the girls on his guitar. Sr. Cortesi, tickled by the idea of an English family forming a serious Paraguayan harp trio, now went a step further; he also offered to teach Terry how to adapt his guitar playing to the rhythms of the girls' folklore music. So we soon had a harp trio that could perform in public.

Not withstanding Sr. Cortesi's reduction in his fee, the cost of the whole enterprise was well beyond the pocket of one on a missionary allowance. There was not only the expense of the lessons but also of the purchase of the instruments – the two harps, the guitar and an accordion which Rosemary had learnt to play. There were the costumes to buy – the girls had authentic dresses trimmed with Paraguayan lace and Terry a typical poncho, sash and high boots. Then the expense of travelling to engagements further afield, such as our flight to the Paraguayan Chaco, had to be taken into account. Clearly, if we were to attempt such a project, it would mean that the whole family would have to accept further stringent economies in our already meagre life-style. But so great was the desire to go ahead that everyone readily agreed to pull in their belts for the common cause.

We had one asset. As a lad Tony had been crazy on all aspects of sport, including athletics. Competing in a variety of events he had, during his school years, been awarded about seventy beautiful, solid silver cups as trophies. At first his mother had these proudly displayed in their home although, I might add, greatly to her disadvantage, as it was a fearful job polishing them! These he had long since dedicated to be used in God's service.

For example, in his early days as a Christian, he had been deeply impressed by a group of missionary doctors who were living among the lepers, seeking to alleviate their suffering. He wished that he also could make some similar sacrifice in his service for Christ, and the things he valued most at that time were his cups! It was the only means he had to make a contribution to help these afflicted people and those who were so valiantly caring for them. So he took his cups down and sent most of them in support of this cause. However, we still had a few stored away in a trunk, thinking that perhaps one day they might be useful for the national churches as chalices in the Holy Communion, but they had proved too ornate for such a purpose. We now felt that our Christian music group, by which we hoped to enrich the lives of others, would be a worthy cause for which to sell them. So I was entrusted with the task of having them valued by a local silversmith. To our delight they realised more than we could have hoped, and so our project got off the ground financially.

Practically all Paraguayan musicians play from memory without any written music; their compositions are passed from one to another through personal instruction. The youngsters loved the music and made rapid strides in learning it from Sr. Cortesi. There are two main rhythms, the polka and the guarania, in both of which the harp plays a 3/3 beat accompanied by the syncopated 2/2 rhythm of the guitar. The guarania is much slower and more plaintive than the polka and has some of the most haunting melodies of all South American music. Most of the tunes are composed and played by the peasant people themselves, who seem to have music burnt into their souls.

These folklore melodies are usually either love songs or descriptive of different aspects of nature or Paraguayan culture. One of the most celebrated harp pieces is called 'Pájaro Campana' (Bell Bird) which starts by mimicking the delicate tinkle of its call. Gradually the music works up to a crescendo as, with perfect precision, it captures the sound of the Paraguayan jungle as it reverberates to the full choir of hundreds of these birds. Other themes are: the water-fall; the limpid waters of Lake Ipacaraí; the local steam-train as it puffs its way jauntily down the line; the sad lament of a maiden abandoned by her lover; the lithe movement of an Indian girl as, sleek as a panther, she glides naked through the forest; the roll of the drums in one of their celebrated battles. These and many more are adumbrated with alluring accuracy by this highly versatile and descriptive instrument.

The Paraguayan harp is quite different from its more conventional Welsh and Irish counterparts; for example, it has no heavy pedals for changing key. This limits it to the major and minor of the key in which it is tuned but has the great advantage of making it extremely light to carry around. As it is built of light cedar and pinewood its total weight is only 12 lbs.

It was originally introduced by the Jesuit missionaries from Spain in the 16th and 17th centuries and adapted by the Paraguayans to its present form. Paraguayan harpists are usually male; they place the feet of the harp on a chair while they stand by its side to play. However, our girls used to play seated with the harp resting on the ground. The sound box, the pole and the head of the harp all fit together without glue; the only thing that holds them firm is the pressure from its 36 strings when tuned.

One of our first engagements after the trio had been formed was at the Mennonite Leper Colony in Paraguay. This seemed so appropriate after Tony's early keenness to help the lepers. We went expecting to be put under considerable emotional strain as we met these poor souls, some of the few in the world that were still afflicted with this terrible, disfiguring disease. But nothing could have been further from reality – we left inspired and humbled by the spirit of happiness and courage radiating from so many of the lepers, most of whom were committed Christians. Furthermore, the devoted care and love of those who attended them also challenged us. The group played many of the old-time favourites from their repertoire of well-known Paraguayan folk tunes. The joy on the faces of the audience was more than sufficient reward as they revelled in the harp music.

We were introduced to several of the outstanding characters in the colony. One of these was a shoemaker, himself a leper. His contribution to the well-being of his fellow sufferers was through the construction of remedial shoes for their affected limbs. The disease had often eaten away the bone, leaving them with grotesquely clubbed feet. Through his skilful moulding of foam, soft leather and plastic he was able to design a special shoe to meet the individual need of even the most deformed patients, bringing untold relief to their aching feet.

Another beautiful character that we felt privileged to meet was an old leper lady. She had her head and part of her face wrapped in a scarf in an attempt to cover up the worst of her disfigurement. On one side of her face her cheekbone had been completely eaten away which meant that her cheek blew in and out with every breath. To some perhaps this might have appeared grotesque – to us she was radiantly beautiful because of her Christ-like character. Undeterred by her disability, even at the age of seventy, she had taught herself how to read so that she could visit her fellow sufferers, read to them selected passages of comfort from her Bible and pray with them afterwards.

We left thanking God for the priceless privilege of having been able to meet these dear people and then to brighten their lives just a little with the beautiful harp music that they had so much enjoyed.

Now we began to think of using the trio in other ways such as a spearhead for evangelism. Tony had been asked to take overall charge of both Paraguay and the north of Argentina. Accordingly he arranged a visit to a new centre that was being started in the small town of Embarcación in Argentina. To get there involved a very long train journey right across the north of the country. This journey took far more out of them than the performance itself! Our colleagues had booked the cinema for our meetings as the largest building available. But even this proved insufficient and each evening we had to have a repeat performance, sometimes two, to packed audiences. As he stood on the balcony looking down at the huge crowds milling about trying to gain entrance, Tony was overwhelmed as he pondered the enormous potential of the group for extending the Kingdom of Christ.

As there was such interest in the message, Tony now decided to offer free correspondence courses to all that requested them. These courses explained in the simplest words one of the books of the New Testament, starting with John's Gospel. For this there was a large take up. The local staff then followed these people up and gathered them into study groups; from these small beginnings a congregation was established.

Another of our projects for spreading Christ's message across Paraguay was the conversion of an outhouse into a small radio station, made soundproof by special padding materials in the walls. There were two sections separated by a dividing window, also soundproof. On one side of this window was the team that operated the equipment, on the other side the artists, musicians and the like with the microphones.

The programmes were broadcast in Guaraní, the language that we felt most united all Paraguayans. At the time we were experiencing a truly extraordinary phenomenon. There was an inspired outbreak of musical talent on the part of a number of members of our youth club. Almost weekly they were composing the most exquisite songs, both words and music. It was just such an outbreak as during the Methodist Revival in England when Charles Wesley had composed his priceless hymns. These songs in Guaraní went out constantly over the air. Obviously our newly-formed group began to play a full part in this radio ministry.

At the end of each programme we offered one of the free correspondence courses we had used in Embarcación to all those that wrote in. The uptake was so big that one of our team, Jean Lorimer, had to be set apart exclusively for the promotion and follow up of these courses.

Eventually Pattie was old enough to join the group as a second guitarist. Only poor little Jonnie was still too young to qualify. However, indirectly he did play a major part. We were all mulling over possible names for the group. Then, one day, Jonnie came rushing into the kitchen. 'I've got a huge secret' he gasped. 'If you and Dad will promise faithfully not to tell anybody I'll tell you what it is'. We both solemnly promised. 'Well!' he whispered, pausing for maximum effect, 'I've found a humming bird's nest! Do you want to see it?' So off we trouped. It was hanging in a creeper on one of the main paths of our mission compound,

right where a constant stream of busy people walked backwards and forwards. When he pointed it out to us we realised why no one else had spotted it. The nest was minute, the size of an inverted thimble. The humming bird nest is so tiny that usually it only has two eggs. The midget chicks then have to sit one on top of the other, only surfacing when it is their turn to feed.

This charming incident reminded us of the beautiful japonica hedge at the entrance to the Quepe farm. It had been alive with brightly coloured humming birds, darting in and out of the blooms as they sucked out the sweetness of the nectar.

When Tony and I were still drooling over Jonnie's discovery of the precious little nest and chicks, one of us suddenly burst out with, 'That's it! The name must be 'The Humming Birds.' The

193

more we thought about it and talked over the idea with the others, the more convinced we all became. In some of our numbers we used to hum along with the tunes, so the name itself had clear musical innuendoes. The fact that humming birds suck out the nectar from the flowers seemed to portray perfectly our desire to extract the sweetness of Paraguayan folk music for the enjoyment of others. Finally, it was very South American; this little creature is unique to the Americas, not being found in any other continent. Yes! Definitely! Thanks to Jonnie, we had at last found our name. And so it was that at last 'The Humming Birds', or in Spanish 'Los Picaflores', were hatched.

Tony and I like to think that Jonnie's HUMMING BIRD NEST encapsulates much of what we had in mind when we built our family home in South America. One of our old-time friends, on introducing the group before a performance, announced them by saying, 'I had the privilege of knowing all the Humming Birds before they were even hatched'. We certainly had the privilege of tending their nest and were now able to enjoy our chicks as they hatched out and began to share our South American music and culture with others.

CHAPTER TWENTY-SEVEN

The 'Humming Birds' fly to Chile and back

CHRISTMAS OF 1965 was one of suppressed excitement for our family. It was now exactly a year since we had bought the Paraguayan harps and Rosemary and Hilary had started their lessons. Terry, with his acoustic guitar was the third member of the trio but Pattie had not yet joined the group. Our friends in Chile had given us a warm invitation to visit them again and to have a two-month tour there, sharing the Paraguayan music with them. Tony had promised that if the kids really applied themselves and achieved a fair degree of skill, we would accept this invitation. This condition had been met so we were spoiling to make the long 6,000 kilometre round-trip to Chile and back.

We were to travel by road in a long-bodied Land Rover, the harps carefully packed in two wooden boxes and strapped on the roof-rack. As there were seven of us along with all our gear it didn't leave much room for luxuries.

On the 28th of December the weather cleared slightly and so we decided to risk going for the last 'lancha' (ferry) across the River Paraguay which formed the frontier with northern Argentina. The river is very wide at this spot and when, at 4.30 p.m., we were half way across a terrific gale blew up and it began to rain again. Then miraculously the stormy skies parted and to our delight we were able to pass down a corridor of blue. It was a happy start to our adventure.

As part of our economy drive, our staple diet was 'Picadillo' (a kind of meat paste) on gorgeous Argentine bread and delicious fruit bought on the way. A small alcohol stove did service to make hot drinks.

Perhaps I should explain at this stage that, trusting in the prowess of the Land Rover, we had decided on an ambitious plan for crossing the Andes by a rarely used southern pass. This ran from Junin de los Andes in Argentina to Villarica in Chile, which was near to our final destination, Quepe. It speaks volumes that, after the experience, we returned by the well-frequented and more northerly pass from Santiago in Chile to Mendoza in Argentina! As our story proceeds I think you will realise why!

As we drove through some of the towns we were a bit nonplussed at the attention we received. Men respectfully doffed their caps and people stood still on the sidewalks as we passed. Someone enlightened us later that the people had thought the harp boxes strapped to the roof-rack were coffins brought in from the country and that we were a cortège on its way to the

cemetery for a double funeral.

The New Year, 1966, dawned fine as we were approaching the Andes. The following morning we found a delightful little spot by the side of the river and, being Sunday, we rested awhile and had a short service of thanksgiving for a safe journey thus far and intercession for the dangerous crossing of the mighty mountain range which lay ahead. This was a prayer most wonderfully answered, as you will learn.

Now excitement began to run high at the prospect of the Andes crossing. In Junin de los Andes, at the foot of the pass, we filled up with petrol. At the Argentine frontier, well into the pass, the young official seemed astonished to see us and asked us in for a cup of coffee to pep us up for what lay before. Our instruments intrigued him and on request we got one of the harps down with the accordion and the trio played for him and Terry sang. It must have been a welcome break in his lonely vigil and he seemed deeply moved.

We pressed on, stopping only to take pictures of the gorgeous scenery, until we came to a swollen river with only a small wooden footbridge. This bridge was no good for the Land Rover and there was nothing for it but to attempt to ford the river. So, while the others crossed the bridge on foot, Tony nervously edged into the water. Gradually it rose until it came high up on the body of the vehicle and we were terrified that it would get into the engine and cause it to stall half way across, leaving us all stranded in this totally isolated place. But once again it stood up to the test and came safely to the other side.

The next hazard was a lake! No fording this! Here there was a board on a post, which had to be swivelled round to inform the 'lancha' man that someone wanted to cross. We waited long and anxiously. At last we saw it set out, a mere speck on the far side. As it got nearer we could see that it was a wooden raft only just big enough to accommodate the Land Rover and our family. Fluttering from the mast was a large Chilean flag, which evoked a hearty cheer from the family at the prospect of soon being back on Chilean soil again. When we were all embarked we looked more like a top-heavy cork bobbing around on the surface of the water than a ferry. The whole contraption was powered by pulling hard and long on a chain which stretched from shore to shore.

Now we really began climbing up the mighty Andes range, the 6,600 kilometre-long spine that runs down the length of the western side of South America. Here our hazards began in earnest. Up and up we went, zigzagging along the slippery earth track that ascended to ever more dizzy heights with no parapet to mark the edge. Aconcagua, the highest peak in the range, is 23,097 feet high – but fortunately this was some distance to the north of us. At times the track seemed little more that a ribbon cut out of the side of the precipice and even the lowest of the Land Rover's eight gears (plus its four-wheel drive) seemed inadequate for such conditions. With due respect to the condor, I don't recall spotting a single one on the journey, but then we didn't have much time for looking up – our eyes were mostly riveted on the bottom of the rocky ravines gaping many hundreds of feet below us.

Our hearts sank as we approached a part of the track where a tree had fallen across it, apparently blocking our path. Did this mean retracing our steps? It was a devastating thought. But with one tyre grating against the cliff side, to our great relief we managed to manoeuvre through the gap, as under a bridge, with not an inch to spare.

To get the family and all our kit into the Land Rover, an extra third person had to be crammed into the front seat over the gearbox; today it was Rosemary's turn to sit between Tony and me. Suddenly, as we were grinding up a terrific incline in 8th gear, the very worst happened. The pressure of her leg as she flinched with every lurch, forced out the lever for the lower range gears and, being disconnected from the engine, we were in imminent danger of rolling back to the brink of the yawning crevasse. Tony slammed on both the foot and hand brakes, but how on earth we ever managed to hold our position while he re-engaged the gear and juggled the accelerator with the side of his braking-foot, we shall never know. It was just another miracle, but I continued to bear the marks of Rosemary's nails on my leg for some time, reminders of the iron-like vice with which she gripped me in her terror.

So far we had seen no other vehicle on the pass, but now, rounding another of these hair-pin (and hair-raising!) bends, we came face to face with a Chilean border-control Jeep. One doesn't usually argue with the police, especially in such an isolated spot, but it was only a single track and to back along those dizzy heights with a load of kids was asking a bit much. Sizing up the situation with incredible rapidity, the Jeep cheerfully whizzed backwards along the precipice edge until it came to a cut-away in the side of the cliff. This allowed us to squeeze past, but unhappily there was no way of going back to thank them – but I think they understood!

Now we passed through the Chilean border control and once again were received both with amazement and great kindness, being treated to cherries all round. The Chilean police (carabineros) just stripped off small branches from the tree and gave one to each of us, laden with the juicy fruit! So refreshed, we reached the customs at Pucón on the shore of lovely, transparent lake Villarica at the foot of its magnificent active volcano. As ever it was belching out smoke from its perfectly symmetrical snow-capped cone. This had been the spot where we had spent several unforgettable summer camps in our Chile days. It was just as if we were home again. The customs passed our stuff without even opening it and we were on our way back to Quepe rejoicing. This we reached at 11 p.m. six days after setting out. Did we sleep!

In Temuco we had a press interview with the local paper, the 'Austral'. The reporter was so taken with the music that he urged us to put on a cultural programme in Temuco during the week and promised that he would give it good coverage in his newspaper if we did.

He was true to his word. The next day a large photo of Hilary appeared on the front page of the Austral billing her as the South American athlete and musician who, with her family, would be playing her harp at the cultural programme that week. They had somehow got hold of the story that Hilary (and Rosemary) had represented Paraguay in the Inter-American Junior Games, competing against the Chilean team, among others. There was also an excellent write-up on the group, explaining both the nature of the music and the spiritual objective of our endeavour. The result was overwhelming. We gave two recitals in the Anglican church and both were packed. At the second, one of our friends, who arrived late, told us afterwards that he was not only unable to reach the door but couldn't even get onto the pavement because of the size of the crowds that were listening outside. This just reinforced what we were already realising, this medium had such potential to bring together people of all ages, sexes and social backgrounds.

Both at Quepe and Cholchol the group played to the patients in our hospitals. Now we visited the prison in Temuco. The response was dramatic. The prisoners crowded round the group until they disappeared from sight, buried in a sea of listeners. Those who could not get near scaled the bars on the windows all around the courtyard to try to get a glimpse of what was going on. Throughout the programme Terry acted as compère, explaining the music and giving its cultural background. Into this he would weave a simple description of the story of Jesus Christ: who he was and what he taught. At the end, he would invite any who wanted to know more, to enrol in one of the simple Bible correspondence courses that had already proved so valuable in Paraguay. These would explain things further. Terry completely won the confidence of these tough prison inmates and to our great delight many enrolled in these courses and apparently were greatly benefited by them.

We now travelled north to Santiago and Valparaiso. In Gomez

Carreño, a housing estate near to Valparaiso, more than a 1000 people gathered each night to listen in the open air. They had built a high platform on a sports field onto which the trio squeezed themselves and their instruments, with a background of palm-fronds to give it a Paraguayan flavour. In the day, Terry and a group of the fellows from the church challenged the local lads to a game of baby-football and won 5-4 with the result that their opponents came to hear the music in the evening. Each night numbers of people enrolled in the correspondence courses, 120 in all, and showed great interest.

In Valpo we went to lunch with Tony Valencia and his wife, Inés, who had organised much of our programme there. Six-years-old Jonnie felt a bit left out of the music side of things. Here, however, he enjoyed playing with children of his own age, including Prissie Valencia. This was in spite of the fact that she had locked him in the loo after he had teased her too much. Little did we imagine that years later Prissie and he were to meet again and marry!

It hardly seemed possible that we had been six weeks in Chile but sadly the time had come for our return journey! We now decided to cross the Andes by the pass from Santiago and this proved to be a totally different proposition to that of the southern pass by which we had come. Nothing on earth would have forced us to attempt that southern pass again! The altitudes and precipices were similar but the road was usually wide enough for cars to pass, with the edge marked by a parapet; there were also other travellers.

As we climbed higher, the old mountain steam train came puffing into sight as it struggled after us up the slope. It brought back waves of nostalgia as we remembered how we had made our journey from Buenos Aires on that train when we had entered Chile for the first time thirteen years before. How much had happened since then! Then we had hardly a word of Spanish between us and our three eldest had been so small; Pattie and Jonnie had not even been born.

Now, as we approached the summit, we opted for the long tunnel that had been bored right through the central peak. This was dual-purpose, serving both the railway and road. It was a bit too 'dual purpose' for our liking as it turned out that there were not two lanes, one for the train and the other for cars, but only one for both.

The tunnel-attendant had an ancient telephone with which he rang up his counterpart at the other end, to find whether the line was clear for us to proceed or not. This was one of those early contraptions with a handle, which had to be rotated rapidly to make it ring. We had had one of these in Cholchol and knew how crackly and indistinct the line could be. To compound our fears, the attendant looked alarmingly frail and hard of hearing for a job like this, not to speak of giving every appearance of being excessively fond of the bottle!

Of course, we could only hear his side of the conversation but it was sufficiently vague to fill us with foreboding. 'Viene el tren?' (Is the train coming?) 'Ehhh! Ya, viene!' (It's coming) Then, 'Ehhhhh? NO viene? Qué dices? No te eschucho bién.' (Ah! It's NOT coming? What did you say? I can't hear well). 'Bueno, bueno, no viene todavía!' (OK, OK. It's NOT coming yet). And then, with quavering indecision, he waved us on.

Tony switched on the headlights and reluctantly nosed his way into the inky blackness of the tunnel. We were immediately engulfed in a tomb-like stillness, as if in another world; only the sound of our engine echoed eerily back at us. Water streamed and dripped from the rock. Our wheels had to run on each side of one of the railway lines on the slippery, wet surface. There was absolutely no way in which we could have avoided a train, or indeed another vehicle, if the old fellow had, by mischance, got things wrong. Further, the tunnel kept curving slightly, preventing us from seeing what awaited us round the bend. At last, after what seemed like an eternity, a pinpoint of light heralded the end to our ordeal and eventually we emerged once more into the sunlight. We now had the long journey across the plains of Argentina and back to the border with Paraguay.

In Chile the papers had been full of the terrible floods raging in the north east of Argentina but we had thought that they would have dispersed by the time we arrived there. We were therefore not prepared for the masses of cars and lorries waiting at the Paraguayan frontier as a result of this flooding. For us, this was serious because the girls had to get back for the start of a new school year. Also our Argentine money had almost run out. Our only hope now was to catch the river steamer, 'La Ciudad de la Plata'. We knew that these steamers were large enough to take the Land Rover because it was on one of them that we had made the journey from Buenos Aires to Asuncion on our first arrival in Paraguay.

Next morning we were down at the river port by 6 a.m. only to find that there was no possibility of getting the Land Rover on the boat. Also every berth was taken. It seemed absolutely hopeless but I pleaded with a junior officer on the gangway who, when he heard of our plight, incredibly agreed to take me, the three girls and Jonnie on board if we were willing to spend the nights on deck. It was the only solution and we gratefully accepted.

So, having waved us off, Tony and Terry set off in the Land Rover. They knew that the railway from Buenos Aires to Asuncion was away some 350 kms to the east and crossed the River Paraná at Posadas, the southern border of Paraguay, on a strong bridge. There was also a ferry able to convey vehicles. All had gone well for about 150 kms but then the mud had got deeper and deeper. Soon they came to a very bad patch where a lorry and a car were sunk up to the axles completely blocking the road. So it was camp-beds under the sky; that is how Terry entered his 21st birthday the following morning – in a swamp in the heart of South America with only the massed choirs of mosquitoes and frogs to serenade him.

Eventually several tractors arrived and opened the road by pulling the lorry and car out with long chains. Tony now decided to have a go under his own steam. With four-wheel drive and double traction he headed for the treacly morass and, wonder of wonders, surged through to the rousing cheers of the many other travellers waiting to get through.

They arrived at Posadas at 11 a.m. and went straight to the port. The water was so high that the main ferry had ceased running. So there they had to stay another six days until the ferry was functioning again. Fortunately they were able to lodge with a Plymouth Brethren missionary family who opened up their home to them.

Once safely over the river into Paraguay they found to their chagrin that the road to Asuncion was closed. This meant a further delay of three days of frustration. At last the police gave the all clear and they set off again. But there were buses and cars marooned up the sides of the road. A lorry was completely submerged in a gaping crater where the road had collapsed; only the top of its cabin was visible. They narrowly escaped a similar fate when, swerving to avoid just such an enormous hole, they skidded and came within an ace of hurtling off the road to disaster. However, they forged steadily ahead, crossed a tributary of the river Paraguay by ferry, and finally got back to Asuncion totally exhausted. There, we greeted them with deep thanksgiving as of course we had been terribly worried about them – it had been eleven days since they had seen us off on the river steamer.

CHAPTER TWENTY-EIGHT

The Humming Birds tour abroad

AT THE end of 1967 the General Secretary of SAMS, Canon Harry Sutton, visited us in Paraguay. Naturally he heard the Humming Birds practising and playing. It was then that plans were laid for a short whirlwind tour in the UK starting in the beginning of January, 1968. This first mini-tour, consisting of a series of rallies throughout the UK, was crammed into a brief four-month home leave. It was so successful that a second and year-long tour was planned for 1970 that terminated with concerts in Canada and the USA.

The first Humming Bird mini-tour

On January 5th we got off to a flying start in BBC's Bush House, London. In the morning we made recordings for the BBC World Service to Latin America and, after lunch, a further recording for the main BBC lunchtime news, 'The World at One'.

The first of our rallies was in the Colston Hall, in Bristol. When we walked into the hall our hearts sank as we gazed out into this vast, empty auditorium. What had we let ourselves in for? Wherever could enough people come from, even to occupy the first two rows? After all, the largest SAMS rally in Bristol to date had been 250 people. 'Please could those two people sitting right at the back', Terry jokingly rehearsed, 'come up to the front row to encourage us!' When the dreaded hour arrived for our entry on the stage we could hardly believe our eyes. In the front row were the Mayor and Mayoress, in all their official finery, and there behind them the whole of the ground floor of the auditorium was packed with an estimated 1,200 people.

Apart from the rallies, we had numerous interviews with the press, plus radio and television programmes to attend. At the ITV recording studio in Southampton we were tickled when Terry had to share his dressing room with Screaming Lord Sutch and next door were Simon and Garfunkle. We also had to make repeated visits to the recording studio where we were making our early Humming Bird records. On top of all this, Tony spent most of his spare moments translating our Paraguayan songs into English for Terry to sing in the concerts and on the records. This was no easy job, as, of course, they had to rhyme in the new language.

We not only had rallies throughout the length and breadth of England, but also in Scotland and Wales. In Scotland we had nine in as many days – starting in Hawick, then Edinburgh Cathedral, on to Dundee Cathedral, St. Andrews, Arbroath, Aberdeen, Nairn, Glasgow, and finally Oban.

In the Dundee area we stayed with some most interesting people, including Miss Pilkington, of the family famous for their Pilkington glass. Terry stayed with the sculptor of the magnificent Robert the Bruce Statue, Mr. Pilkington Jackson. He showed Terry all over his studio and gave him a signed picture of his statue that we still have. Ten days later, on passing by the field of the Battle of Bannockburn, we were able to see this amazing statue for ourselves.

Our rally in St Andrews University was unusual to say the least. It was staged in a brand new college theatre and was packed out with students. It was so new that it had only been used three times, first by the Archbishop of Canterbury, then by Yehudi Menuhen and now by us; and ours was the only one filled to capacity!

Although this rally was a great success there was one unsavoury incident when a small group of Marxist students infiltrated the hall and began barracking Terry as he was speaking. However, in this they had picked the wrong opponent; Terry was steeped in every aspect of the Marxist debate from his university days in South America. He turned the tables on them so decisively that the rest of the students booed the hecklers out of the building.

By the time we reached Glasgow the group were in a state of near exhaustion. Then we were suddenly told that we had another engagement on Scottish TV in the afternoon before the evening rally. By now Rosemary had a huge blister on her finger and we were wondering how long she would be able to play. That night she hid behind her harp during the whole concert in tears of pain. This whole tour had been far too intensive, especially for such a young group; thankfully the organisers learnt from their mistakes and on the second tour this was rectified.

The second Humming Bird tour

Two years later we embarked on our second tour, but this time it was spread over the whole year. Also our touring team had grown as Terry was now married to his Paraguayan wife, Guedy, and their first son was born between our first two concerts and thus joined our entourage. This time our concerts were far more developed, and the crowds significantly greater. For example, whereas on the first tour we had had only 300 at a small meeting in Sheffield, this time, in the Civic Hall, we had 2,000. We performed under the Grahame Sutherland tapestry in Coventry Cathedral and in a number of the other big cathedrals, such as Guildford and Birmingham, even in the crypt of St Paul's Cathedral. One moment we were in a huge rally in Spurgeon's Baptist Tabernacle and the next in Christ Church College Hall, Canterbury to a packed audience, with Archbishop Ramsey and his wife joining in lustily in the community singing of our Paraguayan songs. In Liverpool we performed in the Philharmonic Hall. In Lincoln Cathedral they were preparing for a special service for the St. John's Ambulance at which Princess Margaret was to attend. They were desperately trying to find sufficient extra chairs to accommodate the large crowds they expected. This was providential as, in the event, our rally was packed out with over 1,500 which meant that we had all Princess Margaret's extra chairs filled as well.

In Cardiff our rally was in Llandaff Cathedral. Here we performed under the massive arch carrying the Majestas, the famous Epstein statue of Christ. Our hostesses that night were a group of Anglican nuns. We had been warned that from late evening until after breakfast the next morning they observed total silence. On arrival, a bright little nun opened the door and welcomed us with a card saying, 'Welcome, please follow me. Breakfast will be at eight o'clock in the refectory at the bottom of the stairs'. Having showed us to our rooms she glided silently away. Rather naughtily, I felt tempted to see what would happen if I presented my own card saying, 'Sister Mary has just fallen down stairs and broken her leg'. Fortunately, I refrained.

Next morning, desperately trying to control our boisterous family, we presented ourselves for breakfast. We were met by broad smiles all round, but dead silence. At breakfast I felt so ashamed as the girls kept dissolving into floods of giggles with each munch of their Cornflakes; in the tomb-like silence this reverberated around the refectory like a volley of musket-fire, shattering the stillness.

We had planned to leave early as we had a long journey ahead of us but the Mother Superior wrote on another card, 'Please don't leave before 10.30 a.m. as then we can break our silence. We all want to talk to the family and hear about your work'. So we stayed and had a most enjoyable time as they more than made up for all the silence by chatting away about their different ministries of mercy they performed out in the community in schools, hospitals and the like, during their speaking-times. We were deeply impressed.

Perhaps the real highlight of the tour occurred towards the

end. At this time, there was an immensely popular programme running on Yorkshire Television with a weekly audience of over ten million. Their studios were in Leeds and the programme was being directed by Jess Yates. He is probably better known today as the father of Paula Yates who married Bob Geldof.

When we had our rally in St. George's church in Leeds, the place was packed out with a number standing; among those standing was Mr. Yates! Afterwards he stayed to discuss the possibility of our appearing on his show and he seemed quite sold on the idea. So he invited us to his studios in Yorkshire Television the following day to discuss in detail these possibilities.

We duly turned up, along with our instruments as requested, and were received with every attention. Mr. Yates frankly admitted that he was not interested in our message but assured us that if we would perform on his programme he, for his part, would do all he could to put us on the map and to help us spread our message. He then proceeded to show us around the studios, explaining everything to us in detail. Three days later we were back. After taking a number of still photos of the group we moved into the studio awed by the sheer size of it. Alternating with a massed police choir, we eventually got several numbers successfully recorded and got back to billets at about midnight.

Over the next few weeks we continued recording. By now we felt that we were establishing a really good relationship with the cameramen and other technicians. Early on, there had been constant swearing. Gradually this subsided and by the time we had finished had completely stopped; for which we were most grateful.

Over twenty recordings were broadcast along with such celebrities as Harry Secombe, Gene Pitman and Dr Coggan, Archbishop of York. In the Radio Times, which featured these celebrities, the spiel was all about our group. On another occasion there was a full coloured photo of the group in the Radio Times.

Eventually the interest was so great that they decided to publish a 'Picaflores' (i.e. Humming Bird) record. The final cherry on the cake was when they published a 'Stars on Sunday' Manual. There, along with a wide range of celebrities such as singers Gracie Fields, Bing Crosby and Harry Secombe, actors like Sir Laurence Olivier and Sir John Geilgud, politician Edward Heath and Earl Mountbatten, was our group, with a full-page photo and write-up! This was an extraordinary experience for kids brought up in a school in Chol Chol.

Perhaps the happiest sequel to this tour began at a last minute engagement near to Oxford at a Youth Festival. It was here that, in the providence of God, Pattie first met her future husband, David Dixie. From then on they spent more and more time together as David followed us to several of our venues and love soon blossomed. For some time David had been feeling God's call to South America and he eventually applied and was accepted by SAMS, later joining our team in Argentina where he was based in the city of Salta, a four-hour journey to the north of us. From there he was able to visit Pattie fairly frequently and soon they were married.

Their wedding in Salta was an especially colourful and happy occasion, kindly organised on our behalf by one of our colleagues there. So on Saturday, the 2 Nov 1974, they were married in the old colonial mission centre. The guests were drawn from a wide range of cultures and backgrounds: there were wealthy ranch owners, the regular Argentinean town folk, English and American missionaries, and a lovely group of their Wichi friends who had come down from the Chaco to celebrate with us. One of these, a Wichi lady called Yolanda, had woven a beautiful carpet in purple and yellow depicting a dove descending on the happy couple; this became one of their most treasured possessions. Also the Wichi bishop, Mario Mariño, led the prayers while Tony took the ceremony.

On leaving the UK we still had a short tour of Canada and the USA ahead of us. From time to time, throughout the tour, John Sutton, Harry Sutton's son, had enhanced our playing with his base electric guitar. He now accompanied us and was of great assistance in so many ways, not least in driving the second of our huge long-bodied cars that had been hired from Hertz. We arrived in Philadelphia where an old friend from Tony's days at theological college greeted us. From there we had to drive to New York where, on Sunday, we had to play three times in Stephen Olford's vast central church to big crowds. After Stephen Olford's appeal, at the conclusion of the evening service, there was a huge response with many young people coming forward to express commitment to Christ.

From New York we had the long and tiring journey to Niagara Falls. Of course these were impressive but with respect we felt they couldn't hold a candle to our Iguazú Falls in Paraguay. At the Canadian customs they impounded all our records, to be picked up again on leaving; this was a serious setback. However, it was more than offset by the amazing reception awaiting us in Toronto, organised by the Church Army. Here the Mayor of Toronto, Mr. Dennison, received us with extraordinary kindness. We were asked to play to him and his aldermen in the new, ultra-modern Council Chambers, this before the press and the TV cameras. It was then broadcast over the news that night.

With such excellent publicity we were not surprised at the wave of interest we experienced in Canada. We had a great response from the students in Upper Canada College and a similar one from the Canadian Bishops in the Diocesan Centre. The next day we were in Toronto University, organised by the secular Art's Club. To our amazement the students filled the place and also stayed to listen throughout Terry's very direct testimony. This was quite extraordinary because usually they go in and out, even when pop groups perform.

We were due to fly back to Paraguay from Miami, performing in the main USA towns on the way, including the Billy Graham Centre in Minneapolis. It was an enormous journey for a very tired family! Indeed, we only just made it in time to catch our plane; having handed in the cars to Hertz and completing all the necessary paper work, we had just 50 minutes to wait for our plane; this after a non-stop journey of days! On the last leg of our flight, the plane was nearly empty allowing each of us to stretch out on triple seats and sleep all the way back to Paraguay.

CHAPTER TWENTY-NINE

Dictators and guerrillas

FEW CAN be unaware of the political turmoil throughout South America from the fifties on. You may remember how on my return voyage to Chile, with the children and Aphra Ward, we had docked in Havana on the day before Castro swept to power in Cuba and established his brutal communist regime there. This became a breeding ground for extreme left-wing terrorist activity throughout South America. Che Guevara is probably the best known of these guerrillas. On the opposite side of the spectrum was the military coup of General Pinochet in Chile which deposed the democratically-elected Socialist president, Salvador Allende, and then ruthlessly suppressed all opposition to his military rule. An equally brutal right-wing regime was that of Stroessner in Paraguay where we had been living before moving to Argentina.

While in Paraguay both Terry and Rosemary came perilously near to paying the ultimate price of living under Stroessner's regime. In the early fifties there was a revolution nearly every week in Paraguay and people would joke, 'Who is President today?' With the country close to anarchy, Stroessner's military coup was welcomed by many as it was hoped that he might restore order and progress. This he did, with utmost severity for several years. But, as ever, unlimited power corrupts and so, unchecked by a democratic parliament, things rapidly passed from bad to worse until there was virtually a total collapse of morals, law and order.

With each change of government after a revolution, every

213

post in the civil service changes hands, even down to the postman, so the country splits into two camps; those on the winning side take over all the good jobs, most of those ousted take refuge abroad, many in Argentina. So when Stroessner's Colorado Party swept into power, 1,000,000 of the opposition Liberal Party left the country.

By his marriage to Guedy, Terry had become unwittingly caught up in the political turmoil in Paraguay. Her relatives had been high-ups in the governing party; her uncle, a lawyer, had been Paraguayan Ambassador to the UK and then Minister of Foreign Affairs. With the advent of Stroessner he fell from power, favour and money. However he did still have some friends in high office.

Guedy's grandmother had been a lady of means but with the death of her second husband (by a bullet in a revolution) she had gradually lost several properties. She wanted to leave her one remaining house to her daughter, Guedy's mother, who for many years had looked after her in her old age. But in Paraguayan law you can only leave a small percentage of your inheritance to one person and the balance is divided among the rest of the family in differing proportions. As Terry had paid for a number of major improvements to her house, she knew he could be trusted to keep it for Guedy's mother; so the grandmother sold it to him for a nominal sum in order to secure it for her daughter.

When Tony and I moved to Tucumán, in Argentina, with our two youngest children, Terry and his family had followed us over. There they played a major role in each aspect of our pioneering work, not least in the writing and illustrating of our new self-instructional study books, called SEAN. However, after three years, Guedy's grandmother had died and so they had to return to Paraguay to look after Guedy's mother and to secure the house for her.

The uncle, furious at being denied a share in the house, tried to find a legal loophole by which to invalidate the sale. When he discovered that legally the sale was binding, he arranged with a friend, who was a police chief, to have Terry arrested by the dreaded 'Pyragüé' ('Hairy Feet'), the Paraguayan name for the hated secret police who tortured people to force them to comply with their demands.

Fortunately Terry was out when the police arrived at the house but they left an order for him to present himself at the Police Station the next morning. Not knowing what to do, he turned in desperation to a friend who was a judge of the Supreme Court. He warned him that once a person was taken by the Secret Police nothing could be done legally under Stroessner's regime to extricate him; not even the British Embassy could intervene. Terry would be tortured until he signed over the deeds of the house to the uncle; if he refused he would be maimed for life, if not killed. The only escape was to flee the country immediately. With that, the judge packed Terry, Guedy (eight months pregnant) and their two little boys (4 and 2) into his official Mercedes Benz and drove them himself to the frontier where he had them rowed across the River Paraguay under the cover of darkness and so to safety in Argentina. That is how Terry escaped a terrible fate and came back to continue helping us in the SEAN ministry in Tucumán.

Like Terry, Rosemary had also married a Paraguayan, Tulio Aliende. Right at the end of our time in South America, she too had had a nasty brush with the secret police in Paraguay. She had procured an excellent job as personal assistant to one of the heads of an engineering consortium that was engaged in the construction of a giant hydroelectric dam between Paraguay, Argentina and Brazil. At the time, Somoza, the expelled dictator from Nicaragua, had taken refuge in Asunción. However, four terrorists had hunted him down and assassinated him there. One of the assassins had been a woman of English descent. She had also had connections in Tucumán where Rosemary had previously been living near to us. Stroessner had given orders to his secret police to hunt down those responsible for killing his deposed friend.

One day, on her way to work, the bus was stopped by a number of soldiers with guns at the ready; they started inspecting the passengers' ID cards and asking searching questions. When it was Rosemary's turn, they soon discovered that she was English and that she had once lived in Tucumán. As their suspicions grew, they all began pointing their rifles at her. Eventually they let her go but with warnings that she should be ready for further interrogation. Sure enough, when she got to the office it wasn't long before the police turned up and started asking top management about her background. Fortunately her boss had plenty of clout and so was able to reassure the police of her innocence and there the matter was dropped.

But it was not only in Paraguay that such things happened; it was even worse when we moved to Tucumán in Argentina. Here the military regime was brutally trying to suppress a resurgence of terrorism and popular unrest. This was the period of the terrible purges and the 'desaparecidos' (disappeared ones) and we were caught up in the middle of it. Tucumán, during our years there, was probably the worst hotbed of violence; scarcely a day went by without some further young people, even whole families, of our acquaintance disappearing in the night. For example, the married daughter of the Armenian family who owned our rented flat, and her husband, were left-wing journalists in Buenos Aires. They disappeared one night and were never seen again. In the morning their little two-year-old daughter was found all alone in the home.

We were very friendly with our Armenian landlord family, especially with the son and his young wife who were members of a Christian student group that was very opposed to the atrocities perpetrated under the dictatorship; they were strong and vociferous advocates for social justice. These students would organise protest marches that were anathema to the authorities who in turn clamped down on them.

One day when I was down town shopping with one of our little grandchildren I got caught up in one of these student riots.

These were barricading the streets by the University and the crowd bottled us up as they reeled back before the clouds of tear-gas released by the police. I was terrified, not least for the child. Knowing that we couldn't go forward, I managed to work sideways and, with baby in my arms, I dodged down a side street and so got away, but very shaken.

Our Jonnie was about fourteen at the time and was influenced by the opinions and activities of these older friends. So one evening, unknown to us, he joined them in one of their protest marches. Regrettably, on this occasion the students actually began attacking the police with petrol bombs. Once again, there were counter-attacks with the usual tear-gas, and this time shots were fired. In the backward rush Jonnie got separated from his older friends. That night the others returned home safely, but without Jonnie. We were absolutely desperate. First we phoned round all the hospitals with no result. Now quite late at night, Tony jumped into the car and went to police station after police station enquiring if a young lad was being held there; again to no avail. Jonnie eventually turned up at 5 a.m. in the morning. It transpired that he had taken refuge in the cellar of one of the nearby houses where they had hidden him. There he waited until the coast was clear, when he came home.

Perhaps I should try to explain how this terrible state of affairs had escalated in Argentina to such a degree. The battle had started between the elected Peronist government and the guerrillas. It began to spiral out of control when the army, frustrated by having to fight by the rules, ousted the elected government and declared outright war on anything that even remotely resembled left-wing views. They acted on the principle that Marxism was a cancer and that the only way to make sure of destroying the tumour was to sacrifice and hack out all the surrounding tissue as well. So anything left wing, however peaceful, had to be ruthlessly eradicated.

This of course affected our ministry, especially in very poor areas where even teaching people to read and write was considered a subversive activity. Oscar Lobo had come to the Lord in one of our early evangelistic campaigns. Now he was living in a shantytown where he was pastor of a small congregation. With Terry he worked ceaselessly, aiding people in every kind of distress. Their little Citroen van was in constant use either as an ambulance, hearse or mini-bus.

Oscar was a highly-qualified university student and as such immediately came under police scrutiny for living in such a deprived area, especially as it was a known guerrilla stronghold. One day he was riding on his motorbike from his home to the chapel in the shantytown, when a full military operation ambushed him. They blindfolded him, put him in a sack, threw him in the back of a military van and took him off for interrogation.

He was left in this condition all night, their method of softening a person up before interrogation. In the morning he was questioned by an officer of the regular army and not by the secret police. Unlike many others around him this meant that at least he was not beaten or tortured. However, he was not released because the officer considered him to be too calm and therefore thought he must be hiding something. Oscar tried his best to explain that in fact he was scared stiff but as a Christian he had the peace of God in his life, because he knew that God had called him to help the poor.

By this time Terry and many other friends had formed a prayer chain; they also phoned everybody of influence they knew. After a day of interrogation, the officer took Oscar outside and told him to leave. Oscar knew that this was a frequent ploy used in such cases to explain why the police had mown down a suspect, claiming that he had run away in attempting to escape. So, with his heart in his mouth, fully expecting to be shot in the back, he walked, and walked – and to his astonishment he found that he was indeed free! It was with considerable trepidation that Terry offered to return to collect Oscar's motorbike!

Another time, Terry had been tipped off by a friendly police officer that Oscar had been taken in again, this time by the secret police. He urged Terry to come round to the prison where he was being held. Meanwhile the policeman, who knew the good work that Oscar was doing, had interceded on his behalf to his commanding officer and managed to persuade him of Oscar's innocence; once again this had saved him from being subjected to the routine torture. When Terry arrived he was horrified at the miserable conditions under which the prisoners were being held – they were all jammed together like sardines in a tin and in the most appalling and unhygienic state; it was just like a scene from the French Revolution. Once again, Oscar had been miraculously delivered from the jaws of death.

How Tony and Terry were not arrested we will never know. Both of them were deeply involved in helping the poor. They frequently visited the people in their tiny one-roomed shacks. They sought to teach them how to read and write, they took them to the hospital when they were ill and did all they could to provide their basic needs of food, clothing and simple medicines when these were urgently required. But in doing this they knew they were making themselves into sitting ducks. Miraculously the Lord preserved them to continue this work.

However, we did not entirely escape, but surprisingly our brush up with the authorities had nothing to do with our work among the poor. It occurred on our return from our home leave in England. During this year away, Terry and his family had moved into our flat to carry on our SEAN work there. On our return, he had rented a small bungalow for us in the foothills of the nearby range of mountains; this was only until he could find a place to rent big enough for his family and thus free our flat for us to go back.

We were very comfortable there but a little concerned because we knew that the left-wing guerrillas had taken refuge in the hills above us; consequently the local people were caught between the devil and the deep blue sea. The guerrillas would come down and demand food and shelter from the local

inhabitants. If this was refused they could be murdered but if they co-operated the army blamed them for being collaborators and accordingly took them into custody. As we were not actually in the hills we hoped we would avoid being caught up in this. However, early one morning we were wakened by someone shouting through a megaphone; when Tony went out to see what was happening he discovered that we had been surrounded by armed soldiers. They commanded him to get back into the house but he, mistaking it for an order to advance, suddenly found himself menaced by their rifles pointing directly at him. It was a scary moment but, realising in time that they wanted him to re-enter the house, he stopped advancing and came back inside.

On the bus between Tucumán and Salta, we were only too used to being stopped and searched at gunpoint but this was the first time it had happened to us in our own home. The soldiers burst in and began a thorough room-by-room search and then went up into the loft. As we had considered this loft to be private, we hadn't a clue what might be stored away there. Furthermore, we had never met the owners of the house and so had no idea what their political affiliation might be. We realised that any amount of incriminating material could have been stored up there. If this had been the case, it would have been almost impossible for us to explain it. The longer this intensive search went on the more apprehensive we became. However, eventually to our great relief they came down and departed.

But perhaps the most ugly experience of this kind did not effect us personally; rather it was the elimination of a whole group of young people. We were seeing off several members of the SAMS committee from the airport in Tucumán. As we were saying goodbye a group of soldiers appeared, each with a fierce Alsatian dog on a chain, and ordered us to stand back. We soon realised why – a couple of prison police vans swished past us escorted by armed guards on motorbikes. Through the small barred windows of the vans we could just make out the occupants, a group of young people handcuffed and with their eyes blindfolded. We watched with horror as they were herded across the tarmac and into a waiting plane.

We realised, of course, that this was a group of insurgents that had been captured. We had been told that often such suspects would be loaded on to planes and then dropped out in the ocean never to be seen again. What we had just witnessed was yet another batch of 'desaparecidos'. We could do nothing other than drive away with our hearts sickened by the mindless brutality of the regime under which we were living.

It was in this cauldron of barbarity and hate that God brought SEAN to the birth. In his goodness this has spread Christ's message of love and reconciliation around South America and now indeed around the whole world. How wonderful that such a message of light and hope could ever have emerged from such a hell on earth.

CHAPTER THIRTY

SEAN is hatched in the crucible

WHILE WE had been engaged with the Humming Bird Tour in the UK, our old friend Bill Flagg had been consecrated bishop of the new diocese of Paraguay and northern Argentina. This was the first step in moving from foreign mission to national church that was so dear to us. Tony was finally released from his administrative responsibilities in supervising the mission in this huge area. He could now concentrate on ways to train national Christians for service and leadership, that had always been his chief concern.

So at the end of March, 1971, Tony and I moved from Paraguay to a completely new sphere of service, based in the large city of Tucumán to the north of Argentina. This meant that at first our family was split between two countries; Terry, Rosemary and Hilary stayed on in Paraguay for a while; only our two youngest, Pattie and Jonnie, accompanied us to Tucumán.

At the time, a theological seminary in Guatemala was experimenting with a revolutionary, new educational method called 'Theological Education by Extension' or TEE for short; it had fired Tony's imagination. Most of our leaders were so poor that they couldn't afford to leave their jobs and families to study in an alien environment. This new concept was ideally suited for them because it was an attempt to take the Bible College to the students rather than the other way round. However, the Guatemala-based courses were all on a Diploma or Degree level and so by-passed the majority of our church leaders who only had two or three years primary education.

Tony felt challenged to develop courses that could reach these people where they were academically, as well as geographically and economically. He was convinced that we had to start at the bottom of the educational ladder rather than several rungs up, which would have been out of reach of the very people we were trying to help. Only then could we gradually increase the degree of difficulty and thus lift even the humblest student to ever-higher planes of achievement.

While all this was going on, Bishop Bill Flagg decided to convene an official Diocesan Consultation. This was timed to coincide with a visit by our then SAMS General Secretary, Canon Harry Sutton. On this occasion the bishop ordained Terry as presbyter so he was now officially authorised for his new ministry of planting churches in Tucumán. In this Consultation we also addressed the need to set up an extension programme in the Diocese. There were two suggested candidates for the post of director or principal; one was a highly respected academic who was working in Spanish in Buenos Aires, and the other was Tony, with none of these advantages. It really all boiled down to whether in our situation we needed a degree-level programme or a grass-root's one. Bishop Bill, Harry Sutton and the whole conference opted for the grass-roots programme that would allow all our potential leaders to participate from the start.

Thus Tony was officially recognised as the leader for this new project and could begin to seek much needed reinforcements to speed things up. He wanted colleagues who shared his passion to make top-quality theological training available to the simplest of our national leaders. Accordingly his mind went immediately to Kath Clark in Chile, our co-worker in the Quepe Training Institute, and to Deaconess Liz Richards from Paraguay who had spent many years faithfully working among the Enthlit in the Chaco. Later we also had the help of Arthur Robinson, stationed in Chile. All these dear colleagues still co-operate as Trustees of SEAN International.

This grass-roots educational programme was named

'Seminario por Extensión Anglicano', or 'SEAN' for short. When SEAN spread far beyond the boundaries of the Anglican Church and became an interdenominational and international body, we changed its name to 'Study by Extension for All Nations' with the approval of both SAMS and the Anglican Diocese in Northern Argentina. Thus we were able to retain the acronym 'SEAN'.

One by one, and for different reasons, our three oldest children now rejoined us. Hilary was the first; at the end of May she had come over to study in the University of Tucumán. Terry and his family came at the end of June to plant new churches. Some while before her brush with the secret police that I reported in the previous chapter, Rosemary and her husband also spent a number of years close to us in Tucumán. She had been a great help, especially in typing up the SEAN lessons. In this way, the Humming Birds regrouped in Tucumán and were hugely instrumental in launching this new educational ministry. Although, of course, each had their own family and personal commitments, they threw themselves with gusto into helping SEAN with every spare moment they had. As the courses were all written in Spanish at this time, the fact that our children were totally bi-lingual made their help invaluable; they acted as guinea pigs for testing the lessons and helped with the many time-consuming jobs needed to print and distribute these early texts.

Whereas with their music they had spread the message as far as the UK, Canada and the USA, it gradually became apparent that this new ministry was destined by God to circle the world. I suppose at the time of writing this book, at almost any moment of day or night, students somewhere are opening their SEAN Study Books with eager anticipation of learning more about their Lord and their faith.

Of course, there were huge obstacles to surmount. I've already described the cruelty of the dictatorship under which we lived that was hardly conducive to quiet reflection and imaginative writing. Looking back, we just cannot imagine how this worldwide ministry could have emerged from such inauspicious beginnings, but such was the power and grace of God that it did. So it was in this crucible that God brought SEAN to birth.

Furthermore, we all had other time-consuming work, particularly at the beginning. We especially wanted to help our indigenous friends in the Argentine Chaco by selling their handcrafts in the tourist shops that abounded in such a large city as Tucumán. We varnished and sold hundreds of wooden chairs with attractive seats of stretched cowhides; there were woven goods, sets of toy bows and arrows and other articles. Obviously this was of great benefit to them, providing them with a slender livelihood, but it meant that our time had to be divided between this and SEAN.

We knew that we already had just the source material required for this lower level, in the courses we had used in Chol Chol and then in the Quepe Training Institute, so this gave us a flying start. But this material was chiefly in lecture-form and so needed the physical presence of a teacher to deliver it. The challenge now was to find a means by which it could be transmitted purely by the printed page without the intervention of the writer to deliver it face to face to the students. If this could be achieved, we realised that it would release the programme from physical restraints to spread out to our students in the remotest areas of the Chaco and even beyond.

We discovered that an intellectual battle was being waged between two conflicting systems of educational technology; all the pundits at that time considered them to be mutually exclusive. The first of these was 'programmed' instruction, the second was open-ended group discussion. As we prayed over the approach we should take, Tony felt God prompting him to experiment by marrying these two methods in a single course.

1. Firstly, each student would be given his or her copy of a 'programmed' self-instructional text. From this text they would be asked to cover several lessons a week at home, each student

proceeding at his or her own pace.

2. The second part of the programme would be weekly open-ended group discussion of all the points the students had learned in their home studies. Each group would have roughly five to eight students directed by a group leader. The leader would be supplied with a special Group Leader's Manual with aids to stimulate lively group discussion, etc.

Our task was two-fold:

First: Tony and his team had to write the 'programmed' lessons for home study. To their knowledge this had not been done before in our discipline and on our level, so they had no model to go on. Therefore, before they could write anything, they first had to learn the difficult techniques necessary to write a truly 'programmed' course; these are similar to the logical sequencing used in 'computer programming' today. Fortunately there were a number of excellent books on this science, so they started scouring the shelves of the city libraries for these and then avidly devoured every word of them.

They also worked through several good secular courses that had been well 'programmed' by experts and although not on our subject these gave them a good idea of what would be required. Tony did a course on accountancy and Terry one on how to draw cartoon pictures; from both of these they got many useful ideas which they later used when writing the SEAN courses.

Now they began practising writing 'programmed' sequences and testing them out on each other. Finally they mapped out a draft study book on the Life of Christ, listing all the teaching points to be included in each home lesson. This eventually developed into six large books on the Life of Christ; this course we also called 'The Compendium of Pastoral Theology' and it became SEAN's flagship text. Each of these six books had between 250 and 300 pages and contained about 25 lessons. Each lesson was broken down into approximately 30 frames, most requiring a written response from the student.

Apart from the text, the illustrations had to be carefully

designed and drawn. These were an integral part of the learning process and not just adornment. Because they were aiming at a basic level, they decided that much of the teaching should be done through cartoon strips and pictures. Here Terry played a vital part; he put to full use his new skill in drawing, acquired through the programmed course he had done. His cartoon strips became a major feature; they were so popular that the students couldn't wait for the next instalment!

Once each draft-lesson had been completed, it then had to be tested face-to-face. For this, the programme-writer had to subject himself to the most rigorous self-discipline; if the test-student got the answer to a frame wrong, the programmer, not the student, had to shoulder the blame. It was then the writer's responsibility to detect the ambiguity that had caused the student's error. A new frame had to be written to correct the misunderstanding and then tested on a new student. Only when the frame had elicited the correct answer from at least two new students could it finally be incorporated in the lesson. A new group of students were then asked to work through each completed lesson. Only when 80% of these students had scored 80% in the final tests were these lessons incorporated into the final text.

Second: the other half of the task was to write a Group Leader's Manual with guidance on running the weekly group meetings to underpin each home study book. These gave suggestions on how to correct the students' work and answer any queries, points to stimulate constructive discussion and to apply the teaching in their daily lives and ministry. Although brief, these manuals were an integral part of each course because they turned the lessons from what could otherwise have been a sterile process of learning facts into a dynamic experience of putting these facts into practice.

The last piece of the jigsaw fell into place when we received a generous grant towards our programme. To decide how best to spend this money we consulted with our users; their almost universal request was, 'Please write a course to train our group leaders.' Rather than write a separate course to meet this need we struck on the rather ambitious plan of turning the Manual for Book 1 of the Compendium into a fully programmed Group Leaders' Training Manual. This manual was designed to train a new leader while he or she was actually doing the job of leading the students in their group meetings.

We tested this new Training Manual in the local Baptist Seminary by using both a group leader and students with no previous knowledge of SEAN at all. The results were most gratifying – all his students scored well above the required 80% in their final exam. Now acting as group leaders themselves, these same people returned to their home towns where they each gathered together their own group of students. By using the Training Manual they, too, saw their students achieve the same 80% results.

With this new weapon in the SEAN armoury, the chain that had for so long kept theological education tethered to a central institution with an academic staff had finally been severed, allowing it to soar off into space to wherever there was a need.

CHAPTER THIRTY-ONE

Back to our beloved Chile

DURING OUR last two years in South America we went back
to live in the country of our first love, Chile, to consolidate the
ministry of SEAN. But as things turned out, Hilary was the first
of our family to return there while we were in the UK on home
leave. It happened like this.

In December 1975, Terry and Pastor Oscar received a letter
from the church in Chile asking them if they would look after
one of their members, an electrician, who wanted to seek
employment in Tucumán. So they found him a job in the sugar
refinery. One day, Terry received a telephone call from the police
asking him to come urgently, as there had been a fatal accident.
On arrival Terry and Oscar found to their horror that the victim
was the electrician. Apparently he had been moving a metal plate
over a generator when someone accidentally switched on the
current. Such was the grizzly nature of his death that the police,
even though accustomed to mutilated bodies, wouldn't touch
him. So Terry and Oscar had to prize open his rigid hands from
the metal sheet, straighten his arms and then prepare his body for
burial, while the stupefied police just looked on. Several days
later, when his poor widow arrived from Chile, she insisted on
taking his body back for burial among his family and friends.
Rather than let her travel alone on this long and most unpleasant
journey, our Hilary, now graduated from university as a PE
instructor, offered to accompany her. It proved to be one of the
most crucial decisions of her life.

While all this was going on, God had been preparing the way

before Hilary. Alf Cooper, a young man working for SAMS in Santiago, Chile, had casually picked up one of the 'Humming Bird' records in a friend's house. This had a coloured photo of the group on the cover and he found himself strangely affected by the photo of Hilary. Her beautiful face, framed by her long dark hair, seemed to be smiling out just at him from behind her Paraguayan harp. On enquiring, he discovered that her name was Hilary and that she lived in Tucumán. So great was this attraction, that he even began to plan a visit there!

The very next day, Arthur Robinson, one of our SEAN writing team in Chile, asked Alf if he would accompany him to a funeral in one of the shanty-town churches. On entering, who was there but the poor, grief stricken widow of the electrician. And with her was Hilary, the girl from the record! His heart gave a mighty thump and then stood still!

Hilary got a job as a PE teacher in a local school. Within four months of their first meeting, we were invited to come over to Chile so that Tony could take their wedding on April 1976! This time we had to cross the Andes by coach and on the return journey were delayed for two days until the pass reopened after being closed by snow.

During our second spell in Tucumán, the churches in Germany gave us a large grant towards the SEAN ministry. With this we were able to purchase a spacious single floor building on the outskirts of the city. This gave us much more room for our offices and production work. We now felt that we had found our permanent home but extraordinarily this was not to be. At the same time the diocese in Chile had received an even bigger grant to purchase a still larger building in Viña del Mar for their theological centre. Sadly this centre failed to attract many students so most of the massive two-storey building lay empty.

Just before our second home leave from Tucumán the utterly unexpected happened. Tony was suddenly invited by Brian Skinner, our one-time agriculturist in Quepe, but now bishop in Viña, to consider moving back to Chile to assume responsibility for the small group of students there and to use the rest of the building for the rapidly expanding SEAN offices. Tony was extremely reluctant to accept; his whole ministry in Tucumán had been devoted exclusively to the SEAN level of education. Indeed, he cannot think what could have induced him at the time to leave our lovely premises there. However, once more history revealed that our move had been by the direct overruling of God because, shortly after, war broke out between England and Argentina over the Falkland Islands. It would therefore have been virtually impossible for us to have continued there anyway. Furthermore, by accepting, it had allowed us to sell our SEAN centre in Tucumán thus releasing a large amount of capital for improved equipment and to help fund the translation and production of SEAN courses in many impoverished areas of the world.

Alf was commissioned to come over from Chile to transport us to Viña del Mar. Once more we were destined to cross the mighty Andes Range for the umpteenth time. Alf and Hilary finally arrived to find us in complete disarray. On one hand we were desperately trying to finish our packing ready for the journey, on the other battling to meet our final deadlines for SEAN books that had to be sent to the printers. Finally, early on Transfer Morning, we all squeezed into the van along with what SEAN equipment we could jam into the back. Terry and family were to follow by plane but we took Jonnie along with us.

Our crossing of the Andes was a test to anyone's endurance and took longer than expected. As there were no hotels in the middle of the Andes, the nearest we could find instead was a scrap heap of old rusted and crashed cars. So Alf went off to find the 'more comfortable' cars to allocate to each of us as our dormitory. Of course it gets cold up in the Andes by night but amazingly, in spite of this, everyone slept like a log. Next morning, we made an early, if slightly stiff, start.

We were all touched when, on crossing the frontier, Jonnie who had taken over the driving by now, leapt out of the van, literally fell on his face and passionately kissed the Chilean ground so great was his rejoicing to be back in the beloved country of his birth.

When we finally arrived in Viña at an unearthly hour the following morning everyone was asleep, so we nearly had to spend another night out in the street had it not been for Jonnie's shouting that finally wakened someone who gave us the keys to our temporary home. Next morning we were awakened with a steaming hot cup of tea; starry eyed at being back in beautiful Chile, we just lay back and murmured, 'Paradise!'

Soon the many empty rooms and accommodation in the Theological Centre were teeming with life. With a huge injection of capital we were able to make grants to other countries longing to publish their own editions of the SEAN courses. Again, in the Lord's wonderful plan for this work, we were now able to purchase computers and word-processors that were just beginning to come on the market. I suppose it is true to say that had the Lord not provided these incredible facilities at this vital time in our development, SEAN could not possibly have achieved the massive updating of texts and writing of so many new courses. For this we just praise God.

We were especially delighted that both Terry and Alf have been able to build up their respective congregations with the SEAN courses. Alf reports: 'In Santiago, our churches took off faster than we had anticipated. We needed to teach and train people. Here was where the SEAN materials were simply made for us as if tailor designed to educate our whole congregation'.

Jonnie's confidence that his arrival in Chile would usher in for him the beginning of a new era was more than justified. Within days he had met up again with Prissie Valencia, a lovely Christian Chilean girl. You may remember that he had met her years before during our first tour of Chile with our musical group when he was only six years old – but on that occasion they had squabbled and Prissie had locked him in the loo. Undeterred, he sought her friendship anew and this time his advances were not spurned, indeed they were warmly accepted. Jonnie had been studying to become a dental technician but was still struggling to earn a living. However, by the time we finally left Chile for England, the dentist he was working for had spotted his considerable potential and had sent him to a top man in the USA to learn all the latest techniques. Jonnie just soaked these up.

Some time previously Prissie's parents had also moved to the States, so her father now phoned Jonnie there to ask him if his intentions towards his daughter were serious. As the fervour of Jonnie's reply left him in no doubt, he now suggested that he contact Prissie to ask her to come and join him in the States where they could then get married from the Valencia home. Jonnie sprang into action and so that is exactly how it transpired. We were sad not to be able to join them but overjoyed to learn of the wonderfully happy wedding they were given in true 'Yankie Style', with Prissie's father marrying them. Sadly, only a fortnight after this noble gesture, Tony Valencia died of a massive heart attack, but we were all comforted to know that the marriage had given him such joy and that his whole family had been there to share it with him. With Jonnie's marriage, the last of our chicks had flown the nest.

CHAPTER THIRTY-TWO

How SEAN spanned the world

The Spread of SEAN in Spanish

WHEN WE started writing the SEAN courses, we had a relatively tiny number of our own leaders in mind; it never occurred to us that they might be of use to other denominations, let alone to other language groups. All this changed when in January of 1973 a big conference on Theological Education by Extension (TEE) was convened in Colombia; the leaders of the movement connected with the seminary in Guatemala had organised this. As Terry had been invited, he took the SEAN books that were ready and laid them out on display. This led to a number of denominations requesting to use them in their grass-roots' level throughout South and Central America. Soon these had spread into all the Spanish-speaking countries on the continent.

From Colombia itself we began receiving the most amazing reports of the way God was using SEAN to transform people's lives within the infamous Bellavista prison in Medellín. Colombia is of course notorious for drug trafficking. The barons of the Medellín drug cartel commanded an army of professional assassins. The prison inmates would be offered the alternative – 'Either join us and obey unquestioningly all our orders (for which you will be well paid) or else face death at the hands of one of our assassins in the prison'. As a result, about twenty inmates were killed every month at the height of this reign of terror. Mutilated bodies would be left lying about, some with hundreds of knife wounds; many of these were disfigured beyond recognition, even totally dismembered. Graffiti were daubed over the walls, painted with the victim's own blood – crimson sketches of corpses, knives, guns were seen everywhere. They would even resort to playing football with the head of one of their victims. So Bellavista prison was just a microcosm of all that was hateful and most violent in Colombia – but it was here that God did a miracle.

Oscar Osorio, one of the inmates of this prison, had begun his life of crime as a child; driven by hunger, he would steal from a local shop. This led to taking drugs and soon to dealing in them and finally to violence for which he was in and out of prison. As he later testified, 'For sixteen years I slept out in the streets of Medellín in a drunken stupor'. Then he came to Christ. Never was there a greater change in a person. From a man of hatred and violence he became filled with the compassion of Jesus for those who were still trapped in vice. He never tired of testifying to them of what the Lord had done for him and assuring them that He would do the same for them if they would only let him.

Gradually the murderous inmates began yielding their lives to Jesus and joining with Osorio in proclaiming the Good News of freedom in Christ to the others. Then they got paint and covered over the hideous graffiti with words of Jesus that offered hope to those who would believe.

It was now that they began to use the SEAN courses to build up the new believers in their faith. Their numbers gradually grew until over 300 were gathering together daily to study the Bible. Songs of hope and love replaced the disgusting stream of invective and foul oaths. Bit by bit the killings began to cease until finally they could report that not one murder had occurred in three years. Now the top prison authorities, both the Governor of Bellavista and even the Prosecutor General of the Nation, were convinced. They accepted that the transformation in their prisons was due entirely to the power of the gospel of the Lord Jesus Christ; as a result, from then on they gave it their

full support. Christ had conquered; a pit of hell had been turned into a community for good and God.

But SEAN was, and still is, also being used widely outside the prisons of Colombia. In 1998, Terry attended a gathering of FIET (International Faculty of Theological Education). The curriculum of FIET is 80% SEAN. In all the South American Republics, it works on three levels: the Basic level is all SEAN, the Intermediate is either SEAN or 6 alternative courses and the Advanced level is all SEAN. Legal status had been granted in several countries so that FIET graduates can receive official government certificates, which is a great plus when teaching RE in schools. In some cases, those who complete the FIET programme receive three years credit in the traditional seminaries and so only have to do one extra year of study in residence to get their BA degree. At this gathering Terry got the latest news on the FIET programme in Colombia and its 4,700 enrolled students. The Rector of a large Baptist seminary there had been a SEAN graduate before going on to obtain several major degrees. He was a great supporter of SEAN and was promoting the courses in the seminary.

Through FIET, SEAN is now fully established in all South American countries, and a number of churches led by our students have thousands of members. Tony was especially interested in Ecuador because of his visit there on his way back from Australia. Among their students, 1,500 were indigenous people living in the impenetrable jungle that he had seen on his visit to Auca territory. Many of these had to walk 4 hours to get to their weekly study groups. What a privilege to serve people with such dedication.

Another Spanish speaking country that uses SEAN is Guatemala. We felt that we owed a special debt of gratitude to this country where TEE originated, albeit on a level above the heads of most of our leaders. We were delighted, therefore, when Terry was invited by the Primitive Methodist Church in Guatemala to conduct a SEAN workshop. At the time they had groups studying Book 1 of the Compendium, others Book 4 while others studied Book 2 of the more advanced Pentateuch course. Terry also discovered that several other denominations were using SEAN there.

While chatting with Rev. Francisco Valdés he made a particularly thrilling discovery. Francisco pointed out on a map three places where SEAN had been effective in the city. 'In each of these' he said, 'there is a local church of over 150 members led by a pastor trained with SEAN'. 'However', he added, 'I bet you can't guess where they studied and trained!' When no answer was forthcoming, he continued, 'All three pastors graduated from our best residential Seminary in Guatemala – the local prison!'

It was a wonderful story. Apparently, an inmate called Abelino Guzmán had given his life to Christ. A visiting pastor had then discipled him with the SEAN courses. Soon Abelino became a sort of prison-pastor to a growing number of new believers. The group increased to over 30 and their extraordinary change of life made such an impact for good on the rest of the inmates that the prison officials asked the Ministry of Justice if Abelino could be released on grounds of good behaviour. When the request was turned down, naturally Abelino was very disappointed.

However, God gave another of the prisoners an insight into the purpose behind this rejection. He said to Abelino, 'I think the Lord didn't allow you to leave at this time because you haven't yet trained anybody to take your place as pastor here'. Deeply moved, Abelino immediately ordered SEAN courses for the entire group and set to work training them. Two years later, a number of them graduated from the six books of the Compendium. One of these was Gildardo Molino who was serving a 25-year sentence for the murder of his wife. He was now ready to be Abelino's successor. The prison officials approached The Ministry of Justice again and this time the appeal was accepted; Abelino was released – in God's time – and Gildardo took over his ministry.

Such was Gildardo's testimony that he too was eventually released with only half his sentence completed. But this time, and learning from Abelino's experience, he had already prepared a good successor for himself. So the well-trained Naj Ascalera stepped into Gildardo's shoes. Eventually, all three were released and each in turn became a respected pastor of growing congregations outside the prison and not only locally, they also have outreach teams ministering up in the hills and across their borders.

The Spread of SEAN around the world

The fact that Spanish was the common language of almost all the South American countries meant that our courses could spread freely into all of them without the need for translation. While this was taking place, we experienced another major breakthrough when we were asked to translate the courses into English. It came about through a visit by Bishop Hambidge from Canada. He was eager to find materials suitable for training his English-speaking

Canadian Indians; everything he had seen was too advanced. Then he met Bishop Bill Flagg who told him about SEAN. He, and his wife Denise, made the long journey down to Chile to see the courses for themselves. They were exactly what they needed and so they asked if these could possibly be made available in English. It was a huge task but once completed provided us with SEAN courses in the most accessible language for translation into others.

In February 1973, while we were still in Tucumán, Bishop Bill Flagg moved to become bishop in Perú. Our old pal Douglas Milmine became bishop of a new diocese in Paraguay and Pat Harris succeeded Bill in the remainder of the diocese in Northern Argentina. We had been working towards a separate diocese in Paraguay for so long and at last our dream had come true.

Recognising the growing importance of SEAN, SAMS now took the unprecedented step of allowing us to return to England to work exclusively on our translation programme from Spanish into English. One of our colleagues from Paraguay, Tony Thompson, was building up a new congregation in Milton Keynes. This provided us with the perfect target population on our level to test out the translation. Milton Keynes was also the home of the newly established Open University and one of the Christian lecturers there, Dr. Clive Lawless, took an active interest in our work. Our relationship became so close that at the end of the year he asked us to programme a course on nutrition on our level as the Open University had been asked for this by the Shah of Iran. Sadly, the Shah was deposed before Tony could finish; it did show, however, the confidence placed in our technical ability by these secular experts.

Indirectly, Bill Flagg's move to Perú led to another breakthrough for SEAN. At that time the Christian and Missionary Alliance church on Avenida Arequipa experienced outstanding growth largely among the middle classes. The mission's educational consultant, Dr. Arnold Cook, visited Lima to advise on the training of these new church members and was recommended to contact Bill. He lent Dr. Cook a set of the six books of the SEAN Life of Christ Course (The Compendium of Pastoral Theology). Within two weeks he had gone right through it and, comparing it with all his textbooks and notes from his student days, reported 'It touches on everything I covered at that time'. As a result he became, and has remained, an enthusiastic promoter and user of SEAN. Under Dr. Cook's leadership, the Alliance churches in Perú began using our courses extensively. A city-wide evangelistic campaign in Lima resulted in thousands being converted that were then discipled with the SEAN Abundant Life course. One distinguished visitor reported how on visiting one of their churches on the Avenida Arequipa he found 600 people, many of whom were highly qualified professionals, all studying the SEAN books. He then learnt to his amazement that not far away exactly the same number were studying SEAN in another of their inner city churches. Furthermore, up on the 'Altiplano' (Tableland) there were hundreds of simple peasant folk enthusiastically studying these same courses.

Dr. Cook was later appointed Principal of the Alliance Missionary Training College in Canada. He was so convinced of the value of SEAN for anyone training to go to the mission field that he got all his students to complete the Compendium; only then did he get them to broaden their knowledge with collateral reading. These students took SEAN with them wherever they went and of course translated them into the local language. Many years later, Dr. Cook sought Bill out at the Lausanne Conference. 'Flagg' he said, 'I want to thank you for putting me on to SEAN, that marvellous training pattern. We are now using it in our mission work around the world'. So, without any promotion by us, gradually God spread the news to others so that today SEAN is used in over 120 countries and 70 languages. For example in India alone, the main SEAN courses have been translated into at least 10 different languages. There are now 24 major course books available; along with their group leader's manuals and other supplementary books; this makes 47 volumes in all. Printing runs for a course now range from a few hundred for some tiny tribes and up to repeat runs of 300,000 for one large country.

But the Lord has caused SEAN to grow, not only into many languages, but also into other avenues of outreach. The Abundant Life course is now being broadcast by Focus Radio into many countries, some where few foreigners can reach, for example in the Farsi – Dari language into Afghanistan. Other organisations have adapted the courses for use among the blind in Braille and for the deaf with sign-language.

A relatively new branch of our programme, called 'Train and Multiply', and entrusted to us by its founder Dr. George Patterson, reaches indigenous tribes with a series of 70 booklets in cartoon form. Just one of these T&M users, Thailand, has tens of thousands of students in 800 churches with astonishing levels of church growth as a result. The T&M programme has grown to such an extent that SEAN has shared this ministry with Project WorldReach from Canada, who have up-graded the courses and taken over the production and supervision world-wide.

With our courses now available in so many languages, there is also a growing demand for them among ethnic minority communities. In a foreign land, it is comforting to be able to study the Bible in one's mother tongue. In the USA there are now many more SEAN students studying in Spanish, or in one of the other foreign languages spoken there, than in English. In Britain also, with its multiplicity of ethnic groups, this opens up an entirely new world of opportunity.

As we look back and reflect, we can see that undoubtedly the most valuable and far-reaching phase of our ministry has been SEAN. For this we give the Lord the praise and the glory as it is all of his doing and it is marvellous in our eyes. With our final departure from Chile and return to the UK late in 1981 my story of our ministry in South America comes to an end. However, in an Epilogue I will briefly spell out where we all are today.

Epilogue

MY ACCOUNT of our ministry in South America is told. It only remains for me briefly to tie up a few loose ends as to the whereabouts and ministries of our family at the time of writing.

Terry is now the pastor of a lively congregation in Viña del Mar, Chile and has taken over from Tony as International Director of SEAN and is a trustee of the SEAN Charity. Sadly Guedy died of cancer, but triumphant in her faith in Christ. Terry nursed her to the end. Later he met Alf's sister, Pancha. They are the only couple we've known who actually got engaged on the very first day they met! But it worked; they are blissfully happy and have a wonderful ministry together.

Rosemary sadly had her marriage break down and just recently she was widowed. She returned to England with her two children, worked for 17 years in Tear Fund, eventually trained in Chiropody and is now practising near to us in Seaton. This Christ-like ministry of caring for the aged and lonely, along with her harp playing in many of the residential homes, is a great joy to them and to us. As she now has her own lovely home down town, she kindly keeps a close eye on our garden which she has transformed from a jungle into a perfect haven of peace.

Alf and Hilary are pastoring a large church in Santiago that they planted. It is thriving so well that they now have to double up their services to fit all the people in. Along with Terry, Alf is a trustee and strong supporter and user of SEAN.

Pattie and David were unable to return to South America due to the Falklands War. Their home is in Birmingham where Pattie is now working in the SAMS office. The fact that they are relatively near, means we can still see them more frequently than the rest, who are still in Chile.

Jonnie and Prissie returned to Santiago after their wedding in the USA. Jonnie now has his own lab and is one of the most renowned dental technicians in town, lecturing on the subject even to dentists both in Chile and abroad. The whole family is active as members of their church in Santiago.

Tony and I reluctantly left Chile in 1981 in order to look after Tony's mother who had developed Alzheimer's disease. When she passed peacefully away she left the family cottage in Seaton to us. In retirement, Tony continued for 20 years as honorary editor of SEAN, writing new courses and constantly updating the old ones. For my part, I do all I can to keep in touch with our 5 children, 19 grandchildren and 2 great-grandchildren. Finally, it fell to my lot to write this book.

Further Information

FURTHER INFORMATION about SEAN, or materials or advice, can be obtained from the SEAN UK Office:

    Jacqui Brown,
    SEAN UK, Weycroft Hall, Axminster, Devon, EX13 7LL
    Tel: 01297 630104
    Fax: 01297 630105
    E-mail: admin@sean.uk.net
    Or visit the SEAN website at: www.sean.uk.net

For information about materials in Spanish, Chinese or Korean, please contact the SEAN Chile Office:

    SEAN International,
    Casilla 61, Viña del Mar, Chile.
    Tel/Fax (56 32) 661 484
    E-mails: sean_international@entelchile.net or
    barratt@vtr/net

FOR INFORMATION about SAMS you can contact:

    SAMS
    Allen Gardiner House
    12 Fox Hill
    Birmingham B29 4AG
    Tel: 0121 472 2616
    Fax: 0121 472 7977
    E-mail: gensec@samsgb.org

Why *should* you buy
SIWOK crafts?

Why? Because, each time you buy one of these quality items, you are helping the Wichi indians to survive in their native land in Northern Argentina and preserve their dignity by earning a living wage. Thank you.

SIWOK Crafts
P O Box 7386, Newark, Notts NG24 4WY, UK
sales@siwok.org.uk